Up Your Bracket

Dr. H. Frederick Vogt

Compiled by
Rochelle L. LaValley

Published by Graphic Impressions, Inc./Denver—1977

Third Printing/August 1984

Design and Composition—Graphic Impressions, Inc.

Library of Congress Catalog Card Number: 77-78856
International Standard Book Number: 0-914628-14-3
Printed in the United States of America

Published by Graphic Impressions, Inc./Denver—1977

CONTENTS

PREFACE

Dr. H. Frederick Vogt inspires the many people each Sunday at the Mile Hi Church of Religious Science in Denver, Colorado. This book covers some of the topics he lectures about. Within each topic, parts of different lectures over the years have been combined to give a comprehensive view of his personal beliefs and the teachings of the United Church of Religious Science. The chapters are designed to give the flavor of the actual lectures that stimulated the sudden bursts of laughter and applause, the empathy with a desperate emotional experience and the soaring of the soul upon recognition of life as it was meant to be.

ACKNOWLEDGEMENTS

My deepest sincere appreciation goes to

— Rochelle LaValley without whom this probably never would have happened. Employing all the considerable expertise she has in this field, she took my hodge-podge of stuff and miraculously was able to arrange it into some sort of order and readability.
— My secretary, Andi Hudak, who is not only extremely efficient but cute too (an unbeatable combination), for the long, weary hours in her free time that she labored over a smoking typewriter to get this manuscript ready for the publisher.
— And to my host of friends at Mile Hi Church who have loved me, encouraged me — and kept their thumb in my back!

I LOVE AND BLESS YOU ALL

FOREWORD

First, about the title of this book — I confess I was looking for a title that might cause someone to pick it up out of curiosity.

But there is a deeper significance. It is my observation that most people have "bracketed" themselves in many areas of their lives. They have accepted the fact that they can have "just so much good" in their lives and are trying to adjust to their self-imposed bracket. It is my hope that through the reading of this book, some may develop an inner growth and "up their bracket."

Actually, I have written this book to relieve my guilt. For years friends have been saying, "Dr. Fred, you must write a book" or "When are you going to write that book?" Each time I would feel guilty because I wasn't doing anything about it. So you can see what a relief it is to me to have it finally off the presses.

Another thing you may have noticed. This book is not copyrighted. I have two reasons for this. Number one, if you find anything in this book worth using, feel free. Which brings me to number two: if there is anything worth using, I probably got it from someone else in the first place. Someone said "The way to be original is to read widely and forget the source." Don't most of us do that?

Seriously, I truly hope that somewhere in these pages, someone will find some help, some stimulation to growth, that will have a good and lasting effect on their lives.

INTRODUCTION

For too long, we have made a difference between the "spiritual world" and the "material world," as though they were mutually exclusive. Correctly understood, everything is spiritual including the world of material things. They are all part of man's intended expression. But too often, material things are like ashes in our mouths. They become dry and unpalatable because we're not serene people. These things are nothing unless they are accompanied by a contented spirit and a tranquil heart.

There is a quest for inner peace to calm inner mental, spiritual storms. If you would analyze the prayers of troubled, over-burdened men of all ages, there would be two common denominators: one is asking for outer security and the other is for inward peace.

Modern man seems to feel that he walks along the ragged edge of civilization. He is frozen by his anxieties, torn by emotional conflicts, frightened by economic insecurities, assailed by doubts and cynicisms and fears. He feels vulnerable as he walks along the edge of civilization, and because he does, he searches for devices and techniques that will see him through his life experience some way, with some kind of victorious feeling.

What he needs is not a set of reassuring answers that he can just gobble up, because no such formula exists. Rather what man needs is the inner equilibrium. The spiritual stability that makes man a conqueror in his own time. This is not escapism or a religious cop out, it's something within man that will enable him to live victoriously and contentedly in this present world — where he is right now.

So, when his search has covered all of the exterior sources (material possessions, relationships, circumstances) looking for the key that will calm the storm of his inward being, the circle of his search grows ever smaller until he finds at last that the quest is inward.

This book will help you with your inward quest. As you gain an awareness of your inner being and come into harmony with that, your exterior circumstances will also begin to change. May you find answers and peace here — but never a satisfied contentment. Keep the urge to love, grow spiritually and experience life to the fullest.

1
A NEW LIFE

We sense in life a great mystery, maybe many great mysteries. We feel that if there was some way that we could just loosen up, the result would be a whole new manifestation of our lives and an expression of that which we somehow sense that we are. We feel that there is something back of us or within us that could really make a difference. We could be greater, finer, more effective people. We have a consciousness of a bigger self.

The more deeply we penetrate mind, we cannot exhaust it. When we enter into the world of mind and spirit, we discover a strange and beautiful thing — an inexhaustible resource, a never-failing reservoir.

The great problems of today are not economic or political, but rather they are problems of the soul and of the spirit. The real questions of life are not, "Shall I get rich?" or "When will I find my real true love?" or "Shall I regain my health?" Those are important to us of course, but the real questions of life that you and I are asking are, "What is life all about?" "What am I?" "What am I really?" "What is real?" "What is life?" "Am I meaningful in some way or am I just a happening in a meaningless universe?"

This inquiring attitude is good; it's a healthy mental state. The world, spiritually speaking, is better off for inquiry and controversy since this is how we find the way. Mankind will come up with an answer, a better answer, than has been found today. That answer, in order to satisfy, has to do at least four things.

First, we have to satisfy our intellect; therefore, the answer has to be intelligent. Second, it must satisfy our factual findings to this point, so the answer has to be scientific. Third, it must satisfy our emotions because we are emotional beings. Fourth, it has to satisfy our cosmic sense, so it would also have to be a spiritual answer.

I believe that we are on the verge of the greatest spiritual renaissance this world has ever known. You may look around at our world as it is today and doubt that, but I think this is the kind of crucible in which a spiritual renaissance is born. We are in a position now where each man is seeking to reinterpret life for himself. There are certain things we must know about ourselves. This seeking and finding of something more about ourselves, our place in the universe and what it's all about will cause some change in our established institutions. We've already seen some of those things taking place. I even wonder if perhaps the organized church as an institution could be on the way out to be replaced by something better. There are many changes coming, you mark my word, and many of us will live to see those changes. We're in the beginning stages of those things already.

Throughout the ages, there have been certain people who have plunged beneath the surface of life and found the relationship of the individual to the universal. We've called them "illumined." We may look at those saviors, sages, teachers and gurus and we can interpret what they say, but we will never find a satisfactory answer outside of an immediate, personal, spiritual experience.

In our own way, we are coming to a certain inner awareness that the soul is now already in unity with the universe and with all other souls. There is no separation; there is no difference.

Now is it possible for an ordinary individual to find that inner awareness? It is not just an intellectual experience, but something warm and deep within us that knows. . . and knows that it knows.

There is in this universe a limitless, all-knowing intelligence with infinite capacity to know and to be. Call it God, call it Sam, call it whatever you like. The nature of this infinite being is to express itself. Everything in the physical, material world that we know is expressing itself to one degree or another.

We can say, "Well, it is just a blind, mechanical force that wound up the whole universe to run like this. It'll run down some day." But, obviously, that is not the case and that does not satisfy us, because there is another ingredient in us. We recognize ourselves as warm, pulsating, colorful and feeling beings — we long to love and to be loved, we long to care and to be cared for. Now where did that come from? To me that rules out a mechanistic theory. We are of the nature of this Infinite Being — a warm, personal thing with which you and I can communicate, once we understand where it is and what it is and what our relationship to it is.

"Does God know and care about me?" is a great concern. I believe that God does know me; but it does not know me apart from itself. It knows me within itself as a part of itself and as an integral part. I don't believe I'm God, but I do believe that God is me. You see, when we start from that basis, it changes the whole perspective. As Ernest Holmes said, "All of the life of man is some of the life of God; some of the life of God is all of the life of man; but man is not all of the life of God."

Whatever this life that pervades this universe is. . . that's God. Whatever life you are can only be that life, not different in nature, only different in degree. When are we going to get down deep and not just talk about it, but sense it and feel it until we have a personal, immediate and spiritual experience?

Mind creates. Your mind, then, is the mind of God functioning at the level of your perception of it. There's only one intelligence, and every time you think you are using that one intelligence. Since mind is creative, then your thought would have to be creative.

There are certain things we accept and believe because that's the way it is. We accept certain things about ourselves — right or wrong — and that's the way it is to us until we change what's going on in our minds. The creative Mind is always at work and it can create through us only that which we give it to create.

We can limit or twist or dwarf the activity of that creative power of mind by what we are thinking in our own mind — whether the ideas are expansive, progressive, affirmative or whether they're negative, limiting, circumscribed. This is why our lives are what they are at this point. It is obvious that if we understand this, we can change our thoughts and keep them changed. If we do that, we can change our lives or any aspect that is not satisfactory.

Get it into your consciousness that Life is flowing into everything you do, because that's the only activity that there really is. As you penetrate this greater and deeper awareness, you'll discover that the self is birthless, endless, timeless, eternal, happy, whole, perfect and complete — and so are you.

The great teacher Jesus said, "I am come that you might have life more abundantly." Now, how abundantly are we living? We are here to be and do and experience. We can come to that inner awareness, and as we do, the outer expression matches it — always. We come to the point where we realize that we are ever unfolding into that greater expression of life itself.

We are not here to stumble through this life. We're not here to be mediocre and to fail as often as we succeed. We're not here to rise just to a certain level, to have just a modicum of happiness and fulfillment. We are here that our joy might be full. You can sit and listen to somebody talk like this until you turn blue. . . you can read books until your eyes wear out. . . and it's not going to do anything in particular for you until you actually experience this inner awareness. When that happens, you will find a higher and more beautiful experience in all areas of your life. This new life is different than anything you've ever experienced before.

2
THERE WILL NEVER BE ANOTHER YOU

Since the industrial revolution, it has been a pretty big thing in scientific circles, and some philosophical and psychological circles, to believe that man is nothing more than a machine. The result of a cosmic explosion or a universal accident. To me, that is like taking all of the pieces of a watch and putting them in a sack and shaking them up and dumping them out — all put together as a watch. Besides, the pieces of the watch would have to come from some place originally. In psychological circles, the behaviorists conclude that if you give a man a certain stimulus, he will respond in a certain way. They take a man apart and put him back together again — it's that mechanical.

We foster this mechanical idea in our educational system. We propel our young people along an education assembly line. We label them and stamp them. We teach facts; we have difficulty teaching our kids to think, which is what we should be teaching them. If you were to receive a Ph.D. today, it would have a half-life of seven years. In other words, in seven years or less, half of the material you learned would no longer be valid; and in another seven years another half would be invalid. But along this assembly line the students go, and they come out on the other end with diplomas. A child becomes a group of atoms with a report card.

Science says that if you take all the chemicals in the body, man is worth about $3.94. That's due to inflation — 10 years ago, it was $.98. The IRS has it all figured out how much a man is worth — $750 a year.

We are not satisfied with all that, are we? We feel something within us that is more than that and we cry with the Psalmist, "What is man that Thou art mindful of him, and the son of man that Thou visitest him?" The answer to that question determines our attitudes toward God, society and ourselves. The Psalmist finally concluded that man must be created just slightly lower than the angels. I believe that we will find that he was more right than has been accepted in our day.

Today, too many people think of man as sinful, foolish, corrupt, selfish, evil and depraved. If we think that man is like that, man will be that because we will be what we believe we are.

Don't believe that man is evil. One thing that really disturbs me is the doctrine of original sin, which I was taught from childhood on, and which I think created a lot of the problems that I am now trying to get rid of. Adam, by eating a fruit from a tree, imposed a chain reaction of evil on mankind from that time on; thus, the doctrine of original sin, of total depravity, was created. Would you like to believe and accept that you were conceived in iniquity and born in sin and that in you is no good thing because some person a long time ago did something wrong? Genetically, that's impossible. That's as impossible as inheriting a wooden leg. Perhaps it's more like saying, "I inherited my inferiority complex from my father." This doctrine of total depravity has wreaked havoc upon mankind. It certainly had its place in making people behave and letting the church have full power over them by keeping them subservient in every way.

That doctrine makes God a fool. It suggests that God, who knows all and is all-wise, created man out of Himself, in

His own image, and did not know that man would sin. So now He has to fix up all kinds of punishment for every man from Adam's time. If man is depraved (obviously man did not invent depravity), that depravation has to come from that which created him. That makes God depraved. For what God knows, God is. Who would want to be God-like if God created moral pollution and depravity?

If man is evil, and if that is truly his nature, why does the Bible say that God looked upon what He had done and saw that it was good? That would have to be a masterpiece of Biblical deceit.

What is man? He is variously described as hollow, lonely and enslaved, a puppet, a robot and an automaton. Don't believe those descriptions if you want to make your life into something worthwhile.

Don't believe that the body is corrupt — that the soul is good and the body is evil, as if they were two different things. How could a pure soul live in a corrupt body? People who promote this doctrine regard the physical appetites as being unworthy and wrong. Even food is accepted as a "necessary evil": it's all right to eat, but you shouldn't enjoy it. Sex is a dirty word because that's a desire, and marriage is a concession to that desire. If the body is evil and corrupt, sensory desires of all kinds are unworthy, and we must put them down and wipe them out until we don't desire anything. (Some call that holiness.) In other words, these desires were created only to tantalize us, and only evil people could have and enjoy them — until the rest of us make it to Heaven where we, then, will have all the fun. You do have desires and instincts and can do several things with them. The best thing to do with these desires is to direct them and make them produce something for you.

Man is not divisible. This is a belief in the supremacy of race and of class — that some people are born to servility because of blood and others are born to privilege and power because of the pigmentation of their skin. That kind of thing is moral and social schizophrenia. Sooner or later it has to go, and I think we are making some progress. It's time that we come out of the Dark Ages and recognize that man is man. Man is part of the body of God, regardless of where he is or who he is.

Man is not a pawn on the chessboard of life — shoved around by whim and some supreme design with no choice in the matter.

What is man, then? Man is an incarnation of Life itself. Ernest Holmes said, "There is one Life; that Life is perfect; that Life is God and that Life is my life now." That little phrase will help to make your life better. There's nothing else man could be — there is one life in this universe. Science is saying that one life pervades everything in this universe, and we cannot be separated from it nor it from us, or we would cease to exist.

Jesus talked about the vine and the branches. Break a branch off the vine, and the branch in and of itself has no life, and it dies. Our thought can alienate us if we do not recognize our oneness with life. If we believe some of these things I've mentioned, we are going to alienate ourselves in our own minds from that oneness, and the fullness of that power and presence cannot come through. We may shut it off, but it's still there awaiting our recognition.

If you can think of life (or God) as being intelligence, abundance, love, peace, power and harmony, you can begin

Energy, Light & Information

knowing that you are a part of that life. These are not withheld, they are a part of you already. You don't have to go out and manufacture it for yourself, but you do have to recognize that that is the basis of your very own nature. You can distort this idea of your own life, or you can use it for your own good.

You are good, not evil. Burn that into your consciousness. Get out from under that cloud that has hung over you for far too long and recognize your own freedom of mind and spirit and the fact that you are made out of the life-stuff of the universe. You are created out of the God of this universe, and you are good to the core. This belief can change your whole life experience.

I think a good analogy of how you are related to your body is the relationship of those men in the space lab. They live in it. It has all kinds of fantastic controls and systems, but it is dead in the sky unless they are there manipulating and using it and doing something worthwhile with it. They can do dumb stuff with it — they can destroy themselves and the whole thing — or they can use it intelligently and scientifically.

You live in a body, and it has systems that you also don't understand. The body is not you, anymore than the space lab is the astronaut. You can do anything you like. You can't make it run any better than it was designed to, but you can keep it from operating as perfectly as it otherwise could.

You are in charge of your own life; the controls are in your own hands and you can do something about that life of yours today, right now and every moment. Don't make the mistake of excusing yourself by saying "I'm only human, after all." You are not only human — you are God expressing Himself as you. That's who you really are. If you will know that and know it well every moment of every day until it begins to be the automatic way you live, you will begin to move into a fuller expression of that life that is the real you and has been all along.

I'm not teaching or preaching a doctrine of egotism here; but the fulfillment of your whole life depends on your self-evaluation. How do you expect good things to happen if the person you want them to happen to is unimportant and unworthy? How do you expect others to believe in you if you do not believe in yourself? Who are they going to believe in? The self you wish you were — or the self you think you are. . . but wish you weren't?

You can't have self-confidence if it's built on sand. There's no point in my saying, "You are greater than you think," unless I have something to back that up, unless there is something real and solid to base it on. There is much difference between egotism and conceit as opposed to self-confidence, but that confidence can be empty and unreal unless it's built on some truth that makes sense to you and me. It has to be built on a solid foundation.

For the first time in history, we're coming to the place where intelligent people are setting about to rediscover man. You know why? Because people are becoming afraid of what intelligence, not controlled by spiritual ideas, may do to the human race. Because intelligence has produced such terrible instruments of destruction that worldwide suicide always appears as a possibility. Thinking people are falling back aghast at the thought of their own self-destruction and are searching anew for deeper meanings to life. Even scientists are earnestly searching and seeking for something that will give life value and meaning.

It all goes back to the individual man. Each man is the

center of his universe and that universe will be as big or as small as he decides. Man is the important factor — not society. Society is made up of individuals, and until something happens in more and more individuals, not much is going to happen in society.

Man is a triad. He's physical in that he has an objective body. He is mental in that he has a conscious, emotional reaction to his environment. He is spiritual in that he has a self-knowing mind.

You should know that your thoughts and your word carry infinite power. You should know that you are immortal already. This life that you are goes on forever, ever increasing and ever expanding in one way or another. Yes, you have to learn it; you have to express it; you have to do it — but it has to take place because that is what you are.

There are some practical aspects to the full realization of our own importance in the scheme of things. You see, we haven't known that. We haven't felt important, not really, in the whole scheme of things.

One of the things you'll have to do is to stop selling yourself short. When you know that there is that divinity within you and moving through you, you won't sell yourself short anymore. Oh, how many great opportunities in life we miss simply because we feel incapable. We miss them not because we're incapable, but because we think we are. How much have you thought you were worth? That's where you set yourself and that will be the level of your living.

You won't live on the basis of how you impress other people. When you don't know the real you, you do things like seeking to build a reputation instead of character. You're more concerned with what other people think about you than you are with what you think about yourself. When you seek to build a reputation so that all men will think well of you,

you're encouraging concession, compromise and expedience. You are trying to get by instead of going into the heart of yourself.

The infinite divinity, which was lying in smiling repose within me, one day began to get up and work through me. There was a point at which I turned a corner, I accepted the divinity in me and I have been a different person since that day. I don't mean that that's the end of it, that that's where you quit growing and have now arrived. It means rather that you're growing in a new direction. Something new and beautiful is taking place, but it happens within, then that new awareness goes out to touch and color your life.

Do you respect what you think you are, what you have thought you were, what you have let yourself be? Real success is not in being accepted, but in being self-respected, so you can stand where you are and like who you are and permit that to express itself. Your self-respect encourages others to accept you on your terms. You have a genuineness within you that people can feel. Too many of us live lives that are like movie sets. They look like buildings, but they're all false fronts. We don't want anyone to see behind them because we feel there isn't anything there. When we learn that back there is the real and the front is an expression of that within, we can change our whole life expression.

Know that your nature is the abundance of God, perfect health, winsome personality and successful living on every hand. Feel a growing awareness that you are not alone, because that Father whom Jesus identified as being within, is with you and the consciousness of that presence within will bring a sweet and satisfying, beautiful happiness deep within you and an indescribable glow. It will permeate your entire being, coloring everything within and without with beauty and joy.

You are what you know. You can't be more than that. Thought always precedes act. If you're going to make a chair or build a bridge, first comes the thought, then the physical thing. But there is a whole lot more involved in this because there is more resulting from the patterns of your thought than perhaps we're aware of. Even those of us who may be steeped in this philosophy sometimes forget that our patterns of thought are what is creative in our lives and our experiences. Your life is the result, right now, of the patterns of thought that you have held up to this point.

Our emotions are not controlled by our outward conditions. Nobody can make you mad, but you. Nobody can make you happy, but you. The direction we take or the response we have to our outer conditions, our reaction to what's happening around us and to us, is what creates our consciousness. We can have any kind of emotional reaction we want. I can tell what I think is a funny story, and some of you will think it's very funny and some of you will think it's dumb. I can say something that one person would get angry about and another person would let it roll off. The degrees of happiness, health and success that we experience are controlled by these inner patterns of thought. We can look at life any way that we will. The power of the one intelligence is operative always in those thoughts and in those patterns that we've established.

You are obviously far, far greater than you have known up to this point. We all are. You are now capable of greatness undreamed of in your common hours. You can draw to you all of the experiences whereby life is more and more fully expressed through you. You can do that starting now.

3
FINDING YOUR
TRUE PLACE IN LIFE

We are entering into a new cycle of experience. We see it everywhere, and we read about it everywhere. Those of you who may have read such books as *Future Shock* and *The Greening of America* are perhaps more aware of not only the great changes that are taking place but of the acceleration of those changes that create what one writer has called "future shock." The new psychology, the new science, the new philosophy, the new religion — what do they mean? Where are they leading us? Has the whole "faith of our fathers" been shattered on the rocks of cold science? Has the new philosophy solved the riddle of the universe, or are we lost in a fog of speculative theories? Is there anything really left that is certain? Is there nothing that we can believe, and is agnosticism the best we can do?

There isn't any lack of interest in this kind of thing. Life, hope, peace and love are still dominant factors in our thoughts. We still search for them; we still long for them. God may be dead, but we still long for divine guidance. Immortality may be an illusion, but we still hope that the future does not mean oblivion. Religion may be an hallucination as some would say, but we still have a mystic sense of reality. Science may have failed to find the ultimate cause up to this point, but we still sense and need that invisible presence for help and guidance. We're still asking the same age-old questions: Who am I? Where did I come from? Why am I here and where am I going?

We have to go on; there doesn't seem to be any stopping point. The will to believe is, no doubt, the strongest emotion, the strongest incentive and the greatest source of inspiration to our minds, our souls and our spirits. We might ask, "Can we, by searching, find God?" Some people will say, "Yes, I've found him." Some will say "No" and others "I don't know." And all are sincere. I've noticed that the people who say, "Yes," usually get a little dogmatic about it and feel that their view of God is the only one and their way of finding God is the only way.

You can boil it down to this: the quest of man is after God. To question that means that we are not really acquainted with the human mind. In fact, the quest boils down to two searchings. The first is that we long and search after a unity with spirit, a unity with the presence and an awareness of our oneness until it becomes real to us. The second part of that quest is a realization of immortality. We do not want to feel that we go into oblivion, that this is the end, that this little struggling life we live here for a few short years is all that there is. If we could realize immortality, we would have put down and done away with 99 percent of the fears that plague us in this lifetime. Since there is that quest, the question is this: Can such a universal demand be made without some kind of factual basis in reality? If we have failed in this quest, can it be because we have failed to realize what God and existence means? Perhaps we've been searching in the wrong areas.

There are certain great truths that exist and every one of us senses their existence. One of them is love. Only the one who loves can comprehend the true meaning of love. We've had some strange ideas of what love is; it is not a simple, simpering little emotion but a divine passion that holds us in its grasp and is the driving force of our lives. If we would look for a God of love, we must look deeply and long into ourselves and into each other. We must look away from the differences until we penetrate the unity of the whole.

Another one of these great truths is joy. Everyone wants to be happy. Depression and sadness do not reveal the universe of joy. We fall, too often, to the traitor of indifference and discouragement and we cry aloud to the world that enthusiasm is dead and that hope is gone. We let that be our basic feeling and emotion. A cold analysis is not the answer. The laughter of the universe is not heard when the blood is cold.

Another truth is peace. How can we have peace in our world and in our minds if we persist in remaining in confusion. If our minds are in confusion, we're living a nonpeaceful existence. We cry for peace in our world, but we don't have it in our own hearts and minds. We can't live in peace in our homes. . . and we wonder why there's no peace in the world. We seek world peace by bombing and threatening, or we seek it by something slightly better — negotiation. Even negotiation, if not done by men of peace who are at peace within their own spirits, leads to an empty peace.

A fourth truth is abundance. If ever we would find the abundant life, we must live abundantly. It starts up here in the old grey matter until it becomes an accepted awareness. All good is available to us now — not just some good, not good in some areas and lousy in another — but all good. All the good that is available in the universe is available to you and me right now, but we just can't believe that or accept it, can we? Instead we go out and feel that by our own strength alone we're going to scratch and grab until we gather some portion of that abundance. We limit our receiving by that very attitude because it suggests to our minds that our good is "out there" and we've got to try to coax it to us.

Beauty is another truth. How can we find beauty if we only contemplate ugliness? We can see an asphalt jungle or we can see a beautiful city teeming with life. It's the same city. We can see a beautiful mountain or we can see an immovable obstacle in our way. It depends on our point of view and on what's going on within us.

If we're ever going to realize the eternal truths and express them in great abundance, we're going to have to come more and more into that awareness of the presence of God deep within us seeking to express itself. The Kingdom of Heaven is within us; it's a state of consciousness. We need to meditate and think upon this until it becomes more real to us than anything that the world can present us. We're not here to stumble and fail. Illness, poverty and confusion are no part of God — they are of our own invention.

It has been estimated that man does not use any more than 10 percent of his potential. It's obvious that there are large, undiscovered, and consequently undeveloped, areas within us that have never been probed and have never been released. This can be turned loose by knowing and being within our inner area. We are spiritual beings unfolding into a fuller expression of that which we already are. There are at least four areas that can be developed to promote a greater degree of expression of that God-life within us.

The first one is vision — seeing beyond the visible. We should strive to see our lives, ourselves and our experiences more as God would see them — as whole and already perfect, where the past, present and future come into proper relationship.

The second one is imagination (more than just day-dreaming). This is more than even a subconscious mental faculty; it's more of a superconscious, spiritual faculty that's within us but has to be recognized and developed. Imagination helps us rise above those little ideas we've always had about ourselves which hold us back.

Intuition is the third one. This is a faculty that is available to us, but it's used far too seldom. By the way, history proves that men are just as intuitive as women. Intuition is a direct knowing without any obvious intellectual process. It rises from within, not from our five senses. We become one with all the knowledge and wisdom of the universe. This faculty is one that needs to be more developed.

The fourth area is inspiration. Inspiration really means "to breathe in." The process of being filled by breathing in spirit, intelligence and power is available to us. We become capable of thoughts, ideas, insights, expressions and even deeds that are beyond the usual things that men think and do. All inspiration didn't end when the Bible was finished you know. Men have been inspired from that time to this, and so will you if you will permit it to happen.

The first four faculties are developed by meditation and contemplation. This is the means by which we break the sense barrier. Our senses are so limited, but we are not even aware of the limitations until we break through them. You know what? We're too busy to meditate. Isn't that strange? We are too busy to do the one thing we could do that would change our lives completely. It's not going to happen any other way. I don't care how hard you work and how much effort you put into your living, it will never be what it ought to be because those are sensory things that can only go so far. If we would discover that the most important thing we could do is in the area of meditation and contemplation — tearing down the sense barriers and letting that greater life flow through us — then our lives would begin to change almost effortlessly.

4.
YOU HAD IT COMING TO YOU

How often we say, "Well, he certainly had it coming."
We even say that to and about ourselves: "Well, I guess I had
it coming to me." Now what do you suppose we mean by
that? Do you suppose that long before we knew about the Law
of Mind that there was something that gave us an inner
awareness of the action of the Law of Cause and Effect? It
would seem so.

I remember one time I read in some metaphysical
literature that something wonderful happens to someone all
the time. Nothing wonderful was happening to me right at
that point. I was feeling very sorry for myself for all the
miserable dumb things that were taking place in my life, and
deep inside me I said (almost with a tear), "Why can't that be
me? Why isn't something wonderful happening to me just
once in a while? What is the difference? Why is it happening
to somebody in this world and not to me? Is there a God that
checks over the list and says, 'Okay, it's Joe Blow's turn today'
and dumps a little good on him? and 'No, Vogt, it's not your
turn yet. You may never get a turn'? Or is it just blind luck
(and mine is always bad)? Is there such a thing as fate that we
are all caught up in and some people come out good and
some people come out poorly?"

About that time I discovered the key: You always get
EXACTLY what's coming to you. This is a universe of law.
It's not a universe of chance. Can you imagine what it would
be like if this were a universe of chance? We would have
gravity going off and on and all of a sudden, Ooops, away

you'd go because gravity took a rest, or gravity is working over there but not here. What makes us think that all the natural laws work but spiritual laws operate by chance? We accept laws in all of the other fields of life and we're only beginning to wake up to the fact that there are laws just as real in the spiritual area as there are in any other area of scientific endeavor. We still act as though we feel that it's a kind of hazy thing, at best.

Every part of this life is governed by law. There are even laws in human relations. Discoveries by anthropologists, sociologists and psychologists are finding that this is exactly true. They're not creating new laws; they're discovering laws that have existed all the time. Newton didn't create gravity when the apple fell on his head; gravity had been here all the time.

We have taken and misused the power and the laws of this universe, creating our own chaos and confusion. But the infinite intelligence of this universe, that we call God, is still in control. Once we learn that, perhaps we will get in tune with this whole affair, and life will become a completely different and beautiful experience.

Before you change your thinking, you should take a look at the way your thoughts create your world. "Every thought that one consciously thinks makes an impression on the subconscious mind and that will express as action, according to the strength, desire and belief contained in that thought." The objective mind is the mind that thinks and deals in the world of objects; and there is a subjective mind, which we also call the subconscious. What we think becomes subjectified and goes into the subconscious where it becomes habits, patterns of thoughts and beliefs and memories. The subconscious then reproduces what we think. We experience what we believe and what we think about. If you want to prove it to yourself, look around you and see the state of your affairs.

One time a man said to me, "But I don't know what I believe."

I said, "That's easy. Take a long look at your life, every element of it. Look at your salary. Look at your home — not only the physical structure, but look at what goes on in your home. Look at the state of your health. You will know exactly what you believe."

That's kind of tough because that puts it out there for everyone else to see, too. We like to pretend that we believe better things than that. But our life always levels out at the level of our own mental atmosphere.

The road I propose is not an easy road because it requires mental discipline. We're not used to doing that. Have you ever noticed how our minds run? If you stop and listen, you'll discover that your mind's been thinking all kinds of strange things, much of it negative. We have formed the habit of letting the mind run. Thus making a permanent change in your thinking is like breaking any other bad habit — it takes a while, it takes some work and it takes some effort. If you're going to change your life, you're going to have to change the cause. If you want sunshine, you've got to have the sun because that's the cause. If you want good things in your life, you're going to have to stop wishing and hoping because those are as much doubt as they are faith. You have to go into the area of your own mind and do something about it. It's the old idea: If you plant a radish, you're going to get a radish, even if you thought you were planting an onion. If you want an onion, you're going to have to plant an onion.

Whatever you plant in this fertile soil of your mind, you reap. You are entirely in charge of every bit of that. What your life is right now, you are totally responsible for.

We don't like to accept the responsibility for our lives. We want to blame our mother-in-law, our boss, or our parents who didn't give us the right start. But the fact remains that each one of us is consciously or unconsciously totally responsible for our own lives.

Do you believe that there is a certain element of struggle that man has to go through? That man was born to struggle? That life is a fight? One time I had a sales manager who used to say, "The world is a jungle out there, and you've got to cut and hack and fight your way through it." And that's exactly what he always had to do. It finally got him; he didn't make it all the way through the jungle.

Do you belive that man is subject to and must experience a certain amount of illness, poverty or disease? Do you have a feeling that there seems to be a hand of fate in this world that shoves people around like pawns on a chessboard? If you have any of those ideas, whether they're right out front or vague feelings, yout subconscious picks that up and reproduces them in your life — exactly, without any question whatever and reproduces it exactly in your life. That's why wishing brings negative things. The very wish is an admission that probably it won't happen — so it doesn't happen.

If you don't like your job, your salary, your personal relationships, where your life is going, don't condemn those things because that again affirms them. Plow up the soil of your own mind, pull up the weeds that you have planted yourself and cultivate and plant what you do want. If your life is good in some areas, keep on doing what you have been doing. Find out what your mental attitude toward the good things is and apply that same kind of mental attitude to the areas of life that aren't working.

Are you affirming one thing and getting something less

or something worse? It's very likely that you are affirming one thing and expecting something else. Let me point out to you that if you are experiencing it, you have been expecting it. You have set up the whole thing for yourself.

Start watching what you are saying and then start with the awareness of the power of your word, speaking the most powerful words you can use for your good. Start speaking your word of authority for some good in your life and in the life of others. Speak your good until you feel it and really believe it. You don't have to put the power into the word; it's already there.

Be careful of the power of others' words. Our acceptance of the negative, limiting kind of talk we hear is a tacit approval of that. What do you accept? Are you a garbage pail that allows every negative, limiting, filthy piece of talk to enter into your consciousness and pollute the flow of your life? Do you perhaps have a mental strainer so you can close off yourself from those kinds of things so that it does not become part of your consciousness? It's *your* consciousness that determines the level of *your* living.

If you wonder why negative things keep happening to you, you have to look at what you've been accepting. In the final analysis, what you accept for yourself and about yourself is what really counts and what you will finally experience. The bounty and the good and the abundance of God press in upon you from all sides. But are you letting them in? Your present life experience will tell you. If you're not satisfied with the way your life is going, it's obvious you're going to have to change your mind about some things. You're going to have to put some real discipline upon that mind of yours.

5
HAVE YOU CHANGED YOUR WORLD LATELY?

Did you ever say to yourself, "I wish that I would never be afraid, doubtful, depressed or unhappy again in my whole life"? Did you ever see someone for whom life is going so beautifully that you would like your life to be like that? Did you ever feel that there was something that was almost in your grasp that would make your life more happy and complete?

There are many people today that seem to find that life for them lies somewhere between intolerable on the one hand and unsatisfactory, but livable on the other hand. In order to live in that middle area, we eventually become resigned to feeling that "this is about as good as we can expect." We're not satisfied with it, but we feel that if that's the way it's going to be, we've got to learn to live with it. So we adjust. That's why I don't like the term that psychologists use: well-adjusted. We need to do something more than adjust to the way we're finding life. Within us is the feeling that somehow life could be better than this.

So, we hope somehow for a miracle. By some stroke of luck, things could get better and life could open up. Even as adults, we wish that we had a better job, could own our own business, have a home in the mountains, have a true love and have lots of money. But a wish admits that nothing such is likely to happen unless some fantastic miracle takes place. Wishing is a fantasy world. It breeds discouragement because it actually affirms doubt. There's an outside possibility that it could happen. A wish affirms the belief that we are victims of environment, circumstances and limitation.

Hope isn't much better. Hope is an unconscious compromise with doubt. Yet it's the one thing that keeps us going. The fact that we have a hope that something will get better could lead us to something better. In the meantime, we are hoping and wishing but not really believing; so we learn how to get by.

One statement I thoroughly despise is one that is used far too often: "Don't expect too much, so that if it doesn't happen, you won't be so disappointed." Now isn't that a terrible way to live? Frantically we seek for diversions, trying to make life a little more fulfilling. We seek it in recreation and we save up for a vacation where we can escape into another little world. This is commendable if the proposition were true that this is about as good as life can get. But what a shame and what a loss it is if there really is something we can do to live and experience a better life.

The truth is that there is something we can do. There is no situation that cannot be changed for the better. There is a key that will help to banish forever from your life fear, doubt, insecurity, failure, illness, poverty and bewilderment.

This key is within ourselves. You see, our search for so long was on the outside — never recognizing that we had to go within to find it. We have looked outside as though someone could do something or as though some outer change could take place to help us live that happy and fulfilled life that we desire. Consequently, nothing much happened. This key is within us and is always available — here and now. Of course, we have to get rid of everything within our consciousness that might deny the flow of power in the using of this key.

Your basic attitude toward life is what creates your

world. If you've tried to change your world, and it didn't seem to work, it's probable that you have directed your efforts at the outer aspects of your life and not at the center. If you change some circumstance on the surface but do not change the basic attitude, you'll develop some other problem. So you need to realize that the self is the life, the wisdom, the intelligence and the love of God within you.

All the good that there is, is available. We don't need to merely exist, get by and suffer through. It requires more than a few prayers; it requires a deep change of life, self and attitudes toward life and self.

We smile at the way early man did things. Mankind has always had a religious sense, a sense of the divine. We smile at the way our ancestors used to do things for their gods. They would indulge in praise and appeasement to try to get their gods to help them. The idea was that if they would praise this god enough and bow and tell this god how wonderful and all-powerful he is, maybe he'll like them. On the other hand, in case that isn't enough, they offered sacrifices to this god so that he wouldn't be mad at them. "Here, God, I'll kill a goat for you."

Yet modern-day religion has been doing the exact same thing. Why do we call it "worship service"? What are we worshipping? Is God going to like us better because we go into a church to worship, bow down and tell Him how wonderful He is? Our hearts are glad because we worship Him, and it may really make His day as we worship Him. We also appease God — we sacrifice and do without so God will be happy with us and take us to Heaven on flowery beds of ease. We've appealed to a divine magician and to a heavenly bellhop about as long as we should.

Sometimes we bargain. "If you'll do this for me, God,

I'll do that for you." Every time I got myself in a jam as a boy, I would appeal to God to get me out of it: "I'll serve you forever, and I'll be a missionary in darkest Africa if you'll just help me."

Many people seem to think that prayer is to change God's will so it will comply with our desires and needs as though God really has a tough row set out for us, but if we could work hard enough and get Him to like us well enough, He'd change His mind and not do the kinds of things that He had set up for our lives, as though God's original plan for us is evil. We might get Him to change His mind through so-called prayer.

This infers that the more pious we are, the better chance we have of getting God's ear, and He'll do something for us. Obviously, ministers, being so pious would have the best chance of all. They have devoted their entire lives to this. Obviously, God would listen to a minister better than someone who worked at something else.

A woman came to me and asked me to pray for her son who was in a coma in the hospital. I did so, because at that time I seriously, devotedly, believed in what I was doing as a standard-brand church minister. I prayed earnestly and long for God to please change His mind about that boy. I was sitting in my study one day and I thought about that. I asked myself, "Was I appealing to the divine magician to change His mind? Was that what I was doing? Was I using my influence as 'a man of the cloth'? Was I more holy than she? Did God like me better?"

Sometimes we think that God listens better to beautifully phrased prayers with just the right amount of humility and to six-syllable words all delivered in a stained-glass voice, of course. Have you ever noticed how a minister shifts gears when he says, "Let us pray"?

This kind of prayer did not always bring results, but there is a key that works for everyone. There is a power greater than we are that is exactly alike for everyone. You know that's kind of encouraging because very often we feel a little insignificant. We feel that others are running ahead of us in some way or another. To know that this power is exactly alike for everyone of us helps considerably.

While we are all alike, yet we are all different. It's as though a new mold was created for each of us and life pours itself into that mold. But you notice that the life is the same and the properties of that life are the same. It's merely expressing itself differently because it has poured itself into a different mold. There is no less of it for you than there is for the greatest person you know. That does not mean that man is ordinary. People like Buddha, Jesus and Einstein, who stand out above the crowd, do so because they learned to use the power within. Not one of them claimed to be unusual nor believed that they were. They knew that all people could use the same power.

Jesus, the greatest teacher of them all, came and proved what could be done through faith in this inner power. He didn't say, "I'm more divine than you are," but he said, "You can do this and you can even do better things than this." We didn't believe that. We raised him to a level that he never claimed and said, "Well, he's different; he's divine."

We have to decide that there is a power that works or that there is not such a power, that there is a Law of Mind that responds to us or that there is not such a law. We need to make some firm decisions before we can ever act upon them.

We ought to say something like this to help ourselves: "I am going to act as though this power is really here. I believe that only good can happen to me despite what the appearances might be at the moment. I'm going to believe that everything is possible with God; since God and I are one, everything is possible with me. I am going to believe that Jesus knew what he was talking about when he said, "It is done unto you as you believe."

We can prove to ourselves that there is a power that will work for us in any and every situation of life where we put it to work. We hold the valve in our own hands as to how much of the power is going to flow through us. We can direct and control it.

Use the power within to change your beliefs and your experiences. You're in charge. Take control of your thoughts and attitudes. Don't go around talking about the terrible prices, inflation and recession. Don't talk illness and sickness when you know health and wholeness is the truth about life. Know that that which you hold to and claim is eventually going to be made visible. At the first sign of a negative appearance, don't lose the whole thing. If you become depressed, discouraged, bewildered, don't say, "Well, it didn't work, just as I thought." Jesus said, "Don't judge by appearances." Don't let yourself slip into the feeling that there is such a power, but you're not sure it really works for you or that it works in some situations but not in others. That's a little like putting some of the same kinds of restrictions on electricity. You know the switch is on the wall, but you say, "Well, I know that some people could flip that switch and the lights would come on, but I don't think it will work for me" or "The light worked yesterday when I flipped the switch, but I can't be sure that it will work today."

Fear, discouragement and disappointment can keep us from using the power and from playing the game of life as it is supposed to be played. Some people don't believe that they can be healthy, prosperous and happy, so they're afraid to try, to love, to live life as it was designed to be lived.

The man who is misunderstood and criticized is likely to be doing something worthwhile. The head that rises above the crowd is the one who's going to get the stones thrown at it. We might as well recognize this. Often we have a sense of our own inadequacies, so we're afraid to let our heads stick up there.

Yes, there is such a thing as a game of life, and it gets to be a pretty grim game for too many of us. We're going to have to get off the bench, get out of the stands and play in that game. There's nothing wrong with life itself, you know. The only thing that's wrong is the way we are living or not living it. Quite often, we're not living it to the fullest of our potential. We live our lives according to our belief in life, what we believe about it, what we believe about ourselves and our place in that life. That sets the level. Often we sit back, holler and cheer or boo, and watch life going on all around us and somehow we never really get into the game.

"The authority and the effectiveness of your thought and word rest in the action and the power of the Law of Mind and not in you at all," said Ernest Holmes in the *Science of Mind*. It doesn't matter whether you feel you're too weak, too old, too young. It doesn't matter how long you've been failing to use this power, how long you've been ignorant, how long you've been using that power wrongly, how long you've been limiting it in your life. The very day, the very moment that you change your pattern of thought, the power will change your world right at that point.

You can do it right now, this very moment. It doesn't take any great process. It just takes a decision and doing it. Begin to live it. Despite appearances, you stand there and hold your place until you see the results.

You can use this power in all areas of your life. You can use it to have a pleasant day, improve your bowling, develop a talent, attract a mate, raise your children. You can attract wealth, to become prosperous, and to get rid of a habit you don't need. You can use it to attract the right job, to get the promotion, to invent, to write, to start your own business.

You can use this power for guidance in every iota of your life's experiences. You need to learn to use it. You need to recognize that it is available, that you're always using it anyway. So now direct it in the way you want your life to go.

If you're going to play the game of life — play it. Play it right up to the hilt! As long as you put mental limitations on yourself, as long as you sit in the stands, your life will be limited.

Let me tell you what one boy did. His name is Johnny and I know him well. Johnny is an excellent athlete and had been a star on his Little League Baseball team all summer.

In the fall, he turned out for football and everyone expected him to excell here too. But he had one slight problem. You see, Johnny is deaf.

After a week or so of practice, he came in one day looking pretty discouraged. His Dad asked him what his problem was and Johnny said he might not be able to play because he couldn't hear the quarterback and often ran the wrong play. His Dad thought about it a moment and said, "Now, Son, we know there is an answer and we can have it — right?"

Johnny agreed and went off to his room. Before very long, he came out all smiles and said, "Dad, I've got the answer — I'm going to be the quarterback!" That's exactly what he did and needless to say, he had a fabulous year.

Don't you see that you are in the game whether you realize it or not? Why not play it to win? You have all that you need right now to be a winner and a star in your own right. It's up to you. It's your life.

6
THE PATHWAY
TO IMPROVEMENT

Are there really answers to prayer? Too often people have the idea of prayer as being something that will help you suffer through your problems with little tears in the eyes saying, "I'll carry my burden and I'll bear my cross for Jesus." We'll pray so God will give us strength to bear these crushing burdens. Some people say that prayer makes you feel better, but that's not enough, is it? Instinctively we feel that there should be answers to prayer. How many times have you, like I, said, "Help me," when you got into a tight situation? We feel that there ought to be an answer, but too often we're not really expecting any.

Now if there are answers to prayer sometimes, we need to look at what was involved. If we're not getting answers, we should not blame God, but blame our own ignorant or misapplied use of prayer. There are universal principles at work here, and principles always work the same. So, if one prayer anywhere in this universe has ever been answered and if we can put the right ingredients together, every prayer can be answered.

You can have prayers answered. Instead of prayer, we call it a spiritual mind treatment because we believe that we go at it in a scientific manner and in so doing, involve the principles of this universe.

Let's look at the basic concepts that are important if we're going to get answers to prayer.

1. God is universal spirit. God isn't Big Daddy up in the

sky; God is the life essence of everything there is. There is a subtle intelligence that permeates all things.

2. Man is one with this God and one with everything else. Since everything is made out of the same material, so is man. Since man is the highest evolved of all creation and can consciously use the intelligence that is the one intelligence, man must be most like God.

3. The relationship between God and man is a direct one. It requires no specific formula. It requires no mediator between man and God. The point of contact is in the mind and no where else. Man can't think outside himself, but he can know outside himself. This then gives him the possibility of enlarging his concept and consciousness.

"Well," some people say, "what you're saying is that we're divine beings, we're made out of God." That's right. "If we're divine beings, why are so many people forlorn, lonely, miserable, sick, unhappy and poor?" I'm glad you asked. We have been ignorant of those three basic concepts: God is universal spirit; man is one with God and everything else; the relationship between God and man is an immediate and a direct one.

We need to learn about laws. Obviously, ignorance of physical and mental laws will not cause the law to bend for you. It's a principle. If we use it incorrectly, it doesn't know nor care. It doesn't care how lonely and forlorn you are because you don't understand. It's not going to do something nice for you just because you turned out to be a nice person, because you happen to have read this book or because you went to a good church. This universe is governed and operated by mechanical impersonal principle and law as well as love. God is the creating, sustaining intelligence and that, in essence, is perfection. If it were not, it would have become self-destructive, and the universe would have disappeared long ago.

We are more than just a reflection or a projection of that infinite perfection — we are it, an attribute and an individualization of it. Consequently, there is a pressure within us to be more and more like God.

We are surrounded by and immersed in an infinite law. Maybe we need to differentiate between God the Being and God the Law. Law is a description of how love works, how God the Being operates. Your intelligence is the infinite intelligence flowing through you. It is always creating and making out of materiality that which you think, even if it's not good for you.

The fundamentals of this law are that it has no volition, that it always acts creatively on your thought patterns. You can't fool this law, you can't pretend — it will return to you exactly what you think and believe.

Some people say it's selfish and wrong to use this law to bring good into your life. What is the law here for? Why is there such a law? That's like saying it's wrong to use the laws of growth and nature when you plant a garden because that's for personal gain, personal use. People say that because they think there's a difference between spirit and material. Everything material is made out of spirit in the first place. Everything is made out of God.

We don't try to change reality, we seek to bring that reality forth. We have to learn to think straight, to know the truth despite what appearances are at the moment. We're surrounded by infinite love, givingness and infinite law that can only operate through the channels and avenues of our own minds.

How do you let the infinite law operate through you?

Let me give you five helpful, household hints on how to pray so as to get results.

1. Take a little time to meditate on your oneness with God. Meditate and think about it until you do feel that you are one with everything that is: this includes what you might call God. The reason you do this is because when you get that feeling, it gives you confidence that your word has power. Your word will only have as much power as you really believe. The way to believe that your word has power is to recognize that you are one with everything that is and one with the infinite power of this universe.

2. Speak your word. Don't ask; to ask is like pleading with electricity to come on. If you flip the switch, the current will flow. You can sit there and bawl until you turn blue, but the lights won't come on. You flip the switch by affirming. Hook up with your awareness that you are one with God and then affirm that which you would have come into your life. Affirm that it belongs to you by divine right of birth. It is yours, now, because it is true about you.

3. Let it go. Release it. You see, you are not responsible for the creative process and the resulting demonstration, i.e., answer to your prayer. I could give you a great lecture on the law of gravity and then I could say, "It will draw these keys from my hand to this desk." But nothing happens until I let go. The law with which we are dealing is exactly like that. After you have affirmed and visualized that which you will for your life, you've got to turn that whole thing loose so that the law can begin to operate on it.

4. Be thankful. This is the attitude of acceptance. You're not thankful for something you don't have, so this says to your subconscious, "It's already true." It has to be true in mind before it's going to be true out there in your experience.

As long as you feel need and desire, you have not accepted it as already belonging to you.

5. Keep believing; hang right in there. Be careful not to negate all that you have done in this spiritual mind treatment. Keep on believing until you see the results of that which you have affirmed through this creativity of mind.

Now the subconscious mind. What kind of orders are we giving it, anyway? The subconscious responds to the extent that the idea is believed in the conscious mind. Indecision confuses the subconscious mind where all the action really takes place. Of course, somehow or other, we're going to have to train our conscious minds to be more decisive — to reach a point and make a decision and hang in there. Hesitation and fear of making the wrong decision binds the subconscious so that it cannot reproduce the good things in your life. It causes the subconscious to reach an impasse.

If we're ever going to develop any decisiveness, we are going to have to decide that we're going to decide. True, that decision may be to procrastinate, and a lot of us do that. But if we have done it decisively and decided that right now we're not going to make any decisions, that is a decision. There are times when that infinite intelligence within us will tell us, "Just wait a little bit." But that's a whole lot different than floundering about in the sea of indecisiveness that many of us find ourselves in. If we do it that way, we will be ready to move when it is time for us to do something about it.

Let me give you a few practical suggestions on how to change your world.

1. Decide now that from here on out, you're going to do your level best to avoid thinking and speaking any word of negation, criticism, lack, fear or doubt. You're building a total consciousness here, and the negative thoughts have no

part of it. Throw out of your vocabulary things like "I can't," "I don't," "I can't afford," "I wish," "I want" and "I hope" because you need to develop an affirmative, positive consciousness.

2. Begin now to think about your good. Believe in your own good. Talk like it, act like it, feel like it. Believe in the best, belive in the finest quality, believe in the new instead of the secondhand. On whatever level you put it, that's where your good will be.

3. Smile! You cannot think negatively and discouragingly and smile at the same time. Try it. Smile big and try to think of some unhappy thing at the same time. One of them has to go. When you start feeling down, start to smile.

4. Clean up! An unkept person, house, office or whatever is an evidence of a confused mind, which will not produce what you want.

5. Stop feeling sorry for yourself. I deal every week of every year with people who one way or another are subtly feeling sorry for themselves. Now, that's nice, that's really fun, but it won't get you anywhere. How can you feel sorry for yourself if you know who you really are? Are you feeling sorry for God? That's who you are, you know.

6. Remember that thoughts are things now; thoughts do not become things. When a thought demonstrates itself in the material world, it did not suddenly become a thing. It is the same thing it was before it became visible. So think only of the good, the prosperous, the true and the affirmative until you develop an abundance consciousness, which will then become visible in the material world.

Let's start expecting our total good. Let's not set about to just expect a little bit of good and a little bit of junk. How do you do that? Let me give you six quick pointers.

1. Relax about the whole thing. Being up-tight indicates a fear state of mind. Relax! Let the strain and the pressure go. You don't need them. Besides that, they just make you more ineffective.

2. Recognize that all good already lies on your doorstep, and that door opens inward. Push against it and there's no way that good can get through, while behind you, from the back door, comes all the stuff that you don't want. Realize that all good has already been provided.

3. Dedicate yourself to a statement like this: There is purpose and meaning to my life and I give myself to that. Know that it is now beginning to take place in your life. It's the purpose for which you are here. Have a realization that you are part of this whole universe; you're not a cosmic accident of some kind. You're supposed to be who you are.

4. Identify your ideals. What do you want out of life? What kind of life do you want to live? What do you want to have, be and do? Set those as ideals and become one with them. Hold it to you always. Let that become the new attitude of mind that will change your life.

5. Recognize that the good, which you would have happen in your life, is already true. You don't have to create it, you don't have to make it happen. You can let this wisdom and guidance, which are part of the spirit of God in you, lead you. You can let them bring you to the place where you ought to be at the right time.

6. Act the part of the person living the kind of life you want. Feel it so deeply, know it so well and believe it so much that you can already begin to act and feel as you would when that is part of your experience. You will recognize that you are a citizen in the Kingdom of God and you have all the rights and privileges that go with your citizenship.

This creates an expectancy of good. You have a key born of a new and deeper understanding, of faith and effort. Open the doors along life's pathway to the treasure house of God's good for you. You have your own key; you're not taking anything from anyone else. There is all good available to you now. It's yours. Sense that, and you need never again do without good in your life.

Change your mind, hold it there and keep it changed until that becomes your habitual method of thought. Exactly at the rate of speed and to the degree that you change those basic ideas in your mind, exactly that fast will the outer experiences of your life change.

Now, it's not enough just to think it. You're going to have to reinforce that thought with a deep faith and a deep belief. It's not a random or occasional thought. Calling it up and making a treatment or affirming something nifty is not enough unless there is a deep, firm belief that this is really the truth. To think about it is one thing and to believe it is something else. We need to think it until we actually convince our minds that that's the way it is.

Establish what you can really believe. How much can you believe? When a material demonstration results from that, go from there. Don't nullify your treatment by vacillating. Sometimes we act like a man who builds a brick wall in the morning and then tears it down in the afternoon. We affirm our good, wealth, opulence, affluence and the flow of all good and abundance in our lives and then we sit around and worry, stew, fret and think all kinds of negative things as we look at our lack. Then we've torn down the whole thing that we built in our affirmations.

Stop focusing on and talking about your problem. Who cares about your problem? Nobody wants to hear it anyway.

You notice you lose friends by the bushel if you lay your problems on them all the time. Don't say that your affluence depends on the market, the recession, the inflation or tight money. Quit griping about how much it costs to buy groceries. Just be grateful that you've got the money to buy the groceries. These are all limiting ideas, and as long as you focus your attention on them, you're planting them deeper and deeper into your consciousness.

Stop thinking that it's difficult to have good flowing in and through your life experience. Stop feeling that you don't deserve it. You do deserve it if you're a child of the King, if you're made out of God-stuff. It's here for that very purpose. The less hurried you feel, the faster your good will come to you. Hurrying says to your subconscious that you don't have your good. So your subconscious just keeps reproducing the lack.

Now, if you want to know what you believe (besides looking at your experiences), check your first reaction to anything that happens, especially the unexpected. Is your first reaction, "That's all right, I can handle it"? Or is your first reaction one of panic, anger, frustration or resentment? That's how you can tell how well you've been changing your thoughts and keeping them changed.

I can remember when I was affirming abundance. I was having trouble because I didn't have any money. I'd affirm abundance and the flow of money in my life. Then I'd find myself wondering how I was going to pay the rent at the end of the month.

So often in our lives we get discouraged because we feel we're doing treatments, we're affirming, we say we're believing. . . and nothing happens. We need to look in this area to find out if we are unconsciously denying that which we say we are affirming. We need to establish the end result as we would have it to be in the area of cause — the mind. If we leave it there and do not deny it, it must come to pass.

Our world becomes what we believe about ourselves. Too often we tend to become what we think other people think of us or what they wish us to be. We create this self-image by what we think other people are thinking we are. Each of us has created for ourselves a blueprint in our own consciousness, down to the finest detail. Even though we are unaware of it, we live according to that blueprint. Our thoughts, our talk, our feelings and our behavior are always consistent with this self-image that we ourselves have created.

Any man who believes that he has certain limitations in his life is going to experience them. Life can't go beyond that. The woman who feels that she deserves only so much good or deserves to suffer a little is going to have that happen.

I had a parolee on my narcotic case load years ago who did fine. He stayed away from drugs and crime as long as he had a lousy job and really had to work to make ends meet. But when he got a promotion and things started to go well for him, he got into trouble every time. Something inside him said, "I don't deserve this," and he became uncomfortable when things started going well for him.

I will remind you that life is the creative mind of God in you now and the only limits to the expression of that are the limits that you and I set. We'll always have some limitations, but what we're trying to do is push back the walls.

Shove out the horizons. We can make life bigger, and when we're used to that size of life, we can push it out again and thus increase the quality as well as the quantity of our livingness. Our world will look entirely different to us — a smiling, giving, happy, exciting world rather than the pinched-up thing that it too often is.

7
HOW MUCH CAN YOU ACCEPT?

Every circumstance in life is the result of a definite cause — creative thought and acceptance. It's obvious that no gift has been given until it has been accepted.

We all think we're great accepters, but I wonder if we really are. Did you ever wonder why — after you had thought all kinds of positive, affirmative thoughts and you've prayed, treated and meditated — nothing happened? It might be that you have not yet learned how to accept your good. Perhaps accepting is far more important than we have realized. Because of this ego problem of ours, acceptance is not a developed characteristic, socially or personally.

We think we're good accepters, but suppose your neighbor came to you and said, "Hey, I'm getting a new car and I'd like to give you the one I've been driving." You know what would happen? You probably wouldn't take it or you wouldn't want to. You'd feel very humiliated that your neighbor was so great that he got a new car and wanted to give you his old one.

We have not really learned how to accept. We have mental blocks against accepting because accepting has a subconscious connection with things that attack our little ego. It seems like charity, and charity to us, obviously, is quite humiliating, making us feel second-rate.

It is easier to give than it is to receive. You know why, don't you? Giving make us feel superior and magnanimous and it's something to be praised. But to receive makes us feel inferior, and we can't stand that. It's very interesting — nobody has ever praised a good receiver, have they? "Hey, you're really neat, man, you're really a good receiver." They only say, "You're wonderful; you're so magnanimous in your giving — you're a giving person."

God's abundance is in all things, and it surrounds us now. We've got to know and realize that, but more than that we've got to have an accepting and receiving spirit. If we are not wide open to receive, you can count on it that the universe is not going to force it on us. It's like the air that we breathe: it's available to all of us. We don't have to breathe if we don't want to, but it's there in abundance. It's there to sustain life, but we don't have to accept that if we don't want to. Why then, can we not expand that idea and recognize that all the abundance of God also surrounds us, but the universe is not going to force it on us? It will be ours when we learn to accept it and use it.

We want to be more so that we can do more and have more, but we can't receive because we have this low feeling of self-worth, perhaps at the subconscious level. You see it everywhere, even in the area of love. How many people want love and yet for some reason can't accept it? Right at the crucial point, they'll do something to turn it away, perhaps subconsciously feeling unworthy of love.

We see it in the matter of health. Sometimes we feel that we need to be punished; unconsciously we feel we deserve to be sick, and so we are. Sometimes we can't face a situation, so we let sickness come upon us.

We do the same thing in the matter of abundance. We say things like, "Oh, that would be too good to be true," "I just can't believe it" or "Oh well, it would take a miracle." If we don't feel worthy, it comes out in strange ways.

Let me explain about these inferiority feelings. First of all, let me point out that they're universal. You're not the only one who has them; they're really part of the function of the growing human being. You see, John Doe goes to a social function, and he feels this sense of inferiority, especially if there are important people there. He becomes embarrassed and becomes uncoordinated because he's trying too hard to be someone that he feels he is not.

An exaggerated feeling of inferiority leads to neurotic behavior, and we fight to support our ego. The ego is simply the ideas about yourself that you have collected, and it's always less than it ought to be. Many times, a tremendous extreme ambition covers up a terrible sense of inferiority, a fear of failure.

Learn to be a receiver of good through practice. Absorb the very presence of life, love, wisdom, power, substance just like you accept the air that you breathe and the warmth of the sun. Wherever you go, absorb anything that is pleasant to the soul. Learn to appreciate the fragrance of flowers, laughter, good friendship, a smile, the wag of a dog's tail, the chatter of children. We let so many good things go by without any notice at all. We're so intent on something that we shut out the rest of the world. Practice being an appreciater and a receiver and accepter of the good and the beautiful in life. Give thanks for the opportunity to experience and enjoy everything from the littlest things to the biggest things.

So many of us want to give. The whole world is your field of radiation and expression. But it can only be true when you first learn to receive. There's a flow in this universe; you can't receive unless you give. And you can't give unless you receive.

8
IS GOD INTERESTED
IN RELIGION?

Whatever God may be or whatever God may not be, God can still only be to us whatever we believe God to be. There is this entire possibility that an enlarged understanding of God would and could lead to an enlarged living.

Many ideas have grown up with man about this idea of God. Very often, we still believe in the same God we learned about in kindergarten. Many people who claim to be atheists are saying they are atheists because they don't believe in the old concepts of God that were crammed into their heads. Most of them could rightly accept a higher, better, finer and more truthful understanding of what God is all about.

Obviously, if there is a God, we'd be foolish to deprive ourselves of whatever good that God could bring into our lives. This idea of "I would rather do it myself" could be especially meaningful if we could recognize a greater and bigger God-self about ourselves that would rather do it.

We smile at the childish ideas of God being a grocery man, a general in battle, a doctor, a magician, a policeman or a Santa Claus; yet they're not so different than some of our so-called adult concepts, which man has carried with him for so long. Most of us have thought of God as having hands, feet and eyes and that it's a male with the desire of being praised. He is a church member who belongs to our church and likes people who are obedient to their parents. The Bible talks about all of these things, and we have taken them literally as a picture of God.

One idea that has been quite prevalent is that God is a man of war. He leads us into battle and He's always on our side. We complain, "Why would God let such a terrible thing happen as to lose 50,000 of our fine young men in Vietnam? Then when we pulled out, the country fell apart and went to the Communists." We've laid it all in God's hands and then acted as if we're innocent pawns.

As Rabbi William Silverman has said, "By what right do we drag God into man's worldwide destruction, international butchery and wholesale murder?" Where do we get off doing that kind of thing? It is man who is totally responsible. Man thinks it up and he does it. God is not up there somewhere pulling strings and forcing nations at each other, helping one side to whip the other. We can use the power and the intelligence that is within you and me to do as we please — to bring about destruction upon our earth and into our own lives, or to use it for good.

We've also had the idea that God is "superman" — we have created a God in man's image. This is an arrogant attempt at self-deification without any understanding of what's going on. God then has our human qualities, most of which are bad. We think of God as angry, greedy, jealous, making whopping mistakes, selfish, changeable, being called upon the right way to change his mind, vengeful and so on.

We must reject this old way of thinking! Rejecting an old superstition is not blasphemy and sacrilege; it means that we are on a search for a more mature faith and for a higher concept of God because we need to know.

God and Judgment Day used to scare me. We used to sing a chorus in Sunday School about the Lord writing all the time, seeing all you do, hearing all you say. I thought not only was that mean, but He was awfully busy. If He was keeping notes on everyone, and if He had to keep as many notes on the others as He did on me, He was busy. Then you see, the worst part of it was that one day God would say, "That's enough for the earth." Gabriel would blast the trumpet, the heavens would split open and descending from the sky would be a big judgment bar with God, Jesus and the Holy Ghost. Everyone who has ever lived would have to stand there. They would come out of the graves, the people who were buried at sea would come up, people who have been cremated (all those little particles coming together) and everyone who was living then would stand before that judgment bar. They would be judged according to their deeds, whether good or bad as recorded in the books.

I was glad that my name started with "V." When they got to me, God would say, "Vogt, Hugh Frederick." He'd say to this angel with the good book, "What do you have on him?"

The angel would reply, "Well, not much, a few little items: helped an old lady across the street and a couple of things like that."

Then He would say to the one with the black book, "Do you have anything there?"

That angel would say, "Have I got anything on Fred Vogt! I've got pages!" He would read them, every one. Everyone would hear it — all the things I thought I had gotten away with. (I'll confess to you that there were times when I really was more worried about my parents finding out than God.)

Now I have a different concept. Judgment Day is going on all the time; it is not set for some particular time when the heavens split. Every deed has a consequence tied to it. There is a law in this universe that is absolutely inexorable and it will return your thought to you as experience.

Let's take one more. Man has felt that God is some kind of divine magician. Man has been dominated by fears of one kind or another and he has sought by various means to put the responsibility over on to God and get help from God to alleviate those fears.

First, there were gods for everything: gods of water, fire, lightning, storms, fertility, crops. As man progressed, his idea changed until god became a tribal god. Each tribe had its own god who was stronger than other tribal gods. Thanks to the Jews, eventually, it came down to an idea of one God. But now there was another problem. How was man going to get that one God, who is God of all, to like him better than He likes those others? This God was a sleight-of-hand artist. He would do a little magic for a person if He was approached just right.

Even today, in the days of colored television, satellites, moon landings and all the great scientific things that are going on, we still have a tendency to believe in some kind of magic out of the hand of the infinite God. We invoke God's magic and we call it prayer. We fear God's vengence and we call it reverence.

What is religion? Most people define religion as whatever their church believes. Many religions have many so-called religious rules just as though God were interested. "If you do it our way, God will like you, and if you don't do it the way we say it ought to be done, you're in big trouble, buddy."

Some of them would have us believe that if you don't have the name of God or Christ in the name of your church, you're in trouble. Some would say it's more important to worship on the right day.

The mode of baptism is another point of contention. Should baptism be performed by immersing, pouring or sprinkling? Communion is another one — it depends on who serves, who can receive it and how it's done.

Some churches include in their religion ecstatic experiences of speaking in tongues. Some regulate an external thing such as drink, smoke, dance, outer adornment and drinking tea and coffee. Some say God won't like you if you use contraceptives or abortion.

I know some churches that felt musical instruments in the church came from the Devil and had no place there. Suddenly, though, they changed their minds and permitted musical instruments. Now did God change His mind? I've noticed that the Catholic Church has started having Mass in English. I suppose now we think that God not only speaks Latin but English. Now really, is God interested in all those kinds of things?

If we'll permit ourselves to drop our superstitions and think outside of our particular fences, we would realize that our likeness to God is in the mental-spiritual realm. The Bible said, "God created man in His own image," but then we turned around and created God in our image.

If you are created out of the only life there is in this universe, you are some part of that infinite life that we call God. You are not separated from it. You are to God perhaps as a wave is related to the ocean. A wave is the ocean expressing as a wave. You are God expressing as a person, an individualized expression. Does life or God care what you believe? Not really. The effect is on you — you're not going to affect God by what you believe or disbelieve. You are going to affect yourself and your life with what you believe and do not believe.

There is an evolutionary process going on. The latest scientific findings show that man has been on this earth perhaps four million years. Man has moved steadily, albeit slowly, forward. There is a constant pressure of life within us that wants to be expressed. You can go along with that expression or you can drag along behind, but life will be expressed. You can even run ahead of the pack if you want to. You don't have to wait until all of mankind moves slowly forward at an inch-like pace. By understanding more of who and what you are and your relationship to God and the life of this universe, you can move ahead.

We look at our circumstances and feel that they reflect God's attitude toward us. If our circumstances are good, we think that God likes us. If circumstances are miserable, then immediately we have this great sense of guilt and unworthiness, saying that God is punishing us. We think that our circumstances are an out-picturing of God's attitude when actually they are a reflection of our own attitudes. Your circumstances and mine are earned; most of them we have earned by our thoughts and attitudes. . . and by the reflection of those in our lives.

There is no outside force bringing some circumstances upon you to teach you some kind of lesson. Don't pretend that God or the Devil or your mother-in-law brought those circumstances upon you. There is not a negative condition of life that has not been overcome by someone. This is a universe of law and order; therefore, if anyone has ever overcome your particular problems, then you can. The universe does not play favorites. God cannot change your circumstances until you change them. You change them by what you know, what you're aware of, what you believe and what you will accept.

Whenever Jesus talked about the will of the Father, he related it to living more fully and more abundantly in all aspects of life. He tried to show in so many ways that man's basic beliefs and attitudes were creative. This was so sensible and so simple that it just obviously could not be true for us; it had to be more complicated. So man began to form creeds and mysterious ideologies and to worship the teacher instead of following the teaching.

Actually, what Jesus was saying was that Heaven and God are within man. He indicated that guidance is available. You don't have to wonder what you ought to do on some particular occasion because there is infinite guidance waiting to help you. There is power in the law to do that which you have accepted in your basic attitudes. If you follow those principles, you will find that man has infinite possibilities.

Let me tell you a story I heard years ago. There were two countries, one called the Land of Bliss and the other the Land of Woe. The Land of Bliss was overflowing with abundance. Everyone was happy, healthy, successful and fulfilled. Love, peace, joy and harmony were the order of the day in the Land of Bliss. The Land of Woe was exactly the opposite. There was never enough and there was anger, fighting, discouragement and darkness in the Land of Woe. These two lands were separated by a swift, roaring river, and anyone who sought to cross from the Land of Woe to the Land of Bliss never made it.

Then there came a young man, healthy, strong and vigorous. Because of his love for people, he decided to place a rope across that river from the Land of Woe so people could hang on to it and make their way across to the Land of Bliss. He made the attempt and almost got swept away, but finally by battling the tremendous tide with great strength and agility, he was able to make it to the other shore. The natives, seeing him, thought he was some kind of fierce fish and they shot arrows into him. Just as he was dying, he managed with his last breath to fasten that rope securely on that other shore, and then he died.

When the people of the Land of Woe saw what he had done, they began to worship him as a hero. They said, "Oh, such a tremendous man; he died to save us from this Land of Woe." But hardly anyone tried to use the rope. So, in the course of time, the rope was pretty much forgotten, and it was covered with debris. But the worship of the young man continued. They built monuments to him; they wrote songs about him; they even prayed to him. Then, great arguments began to spring up as to what form they ought to use to worship this fantastic hero. For generations this went on.

Then a body of men got together and said, "Look, why all this strife? All we need to do is worship him as a god. If we will just believe that he died crossing that river in order to save us, then when we die, our souls will float across to the Land of Bliss." That simplified it, and they didn't have to do much of anything.

Meanwhile, the spirit of the hero looked on with sadness. He said, "Oh, you do err, for I *lived* to save you. My death was but an incident in my attempt and death can never be the cause of your salvation. To what purpose was this whole thing if you have forgotten I died while placing the rope there for you. I still love you and still have great concern for you, but I can never carry you across the river no matter how much you implore. You must use the means provided if you will ever cross from the Land of Woe to the Land of Bliss."

But as the hero spoke to them thus, they were praying and arguing so loudly that they could not hear that still, small voice and so they continued to live in the Land of Woe.

Use that rope. Enter the awareness of the power and presence of God. Know that the infinite God is the sum total of all things — past, present and future and contains all knowledge and all wisdom; the infinite is one and indivisible. Take God out of the sky, take off his beard, arms and legs and put Him back inside you where He has been all along.

How are you going to approach that God, that intelligence, that life? Obviously, it has to be done consciously, but there is no one formula. It should be direct and it should be with an acceptance that there will be a direct response. That presence and that power is everywhere. There is no more or less of it where you are than anywhere in this universe. Some places are better for us, perhaps, but wherever you are, there is all the presence and all the power that you could ever need to change your life and keep it changed.

9
THE DEVIL MADE ME DO IT

A belief in the Devil has been influencing many people and limiting their lives.

The story goes that there was this big rebellion up in Heaven. God created many angels and one of them got a little too big for his britches. He led a rebellion, and finally God couldn't take it anymore. God cast Lucifer out of Heaven. He fell through space, and — wouldn't you know it? — he had to land on the planet Earth. Now the Devil is in a battle with God to see who can win the most people.

If you would believe the theology of the people who believe what I've just said, the Devil's winning more than God. In fact, God is not winning very many battles at all. God is all-wise, yet He didn't know that He was creating a monster right in His own midst. Then God put him on Earth to bother us and didn't know that the Devil would win the most souls. You can see what that belief does to someone's consciousness, can't you?

Originally, man attributed everything that he couldn't account for to a god or gods. He also came up with the idea of a devil and "evil spirits." God could be kindly one moment and angry at you the next, but the Devil was never nice to you at all. See where you are now? You're really trapped because you could have God mad at you and the Devil working on you at the same time.

We know the struggle of good versus evil that goes on in man's life. We are not looking at two mighty powers fighting against each other. The fact that the universe is still here and has not yet destroyed itself would indicate to us that there can't be two contradicting powers in this universe.

The Devil is man's personification of his own ignorance of the universe. Man has, one way or another, attributed just about everything bad that has happened to him to the Devil or to evil spirits. There was a time when illness was caused by the Devil. Man developed medicines that have wiped out many of the illnesses that were so prevalent, and the Devil didn't have anything to say about it. Famine was the Devil's work, but man learned how to irrigate and scientifically to grow better crops. So it wasn't the Devil who caused all the trouble, it was man's ignorance.

When people attribute trouble in their lives to some supernatural power, they abdicate their own responsibilities and power to change things. There is no outside force causing you to behave the way you do, you do that to yourself. You and I choose for ourselves the types and levels of our own life expression. Obviously, if we do it, we can change it. But if we can lay the blame on the Devil, we are relieved of responsibility. It doesn't change the situation any — in fact, no change can occur — but at least we're out from under the responsibility of having to do anything about it.

If there is darkness in some area of your life, don't shirk the responsibility. The one power and presence in the universe is available to you, and you can use it to change darkness into light in your own life.

What kinds of devils do you have in your life? There is the devil of doubt. Doubt, first of all, about God. Consequently, immediately there's a limitation of life. Great self-doubt creeps in and we have a sneaky feeling of inadequacy. This self-doubt causes the devil of bad temper.

Doubt leads to another devil — guilt. My wife says, "I

do the laundry because I'd feel guilty if my family didn't have nice, clean clothes to wear. I clean the house because I'd feel guilty if my family had to live in clutter. I prepare nice, tasty meals because I would feel terribly guilty if my family didn't have good food to eat. In fact, I owe all my happiness to guilt."

Who feels guilty? The rich feel guilty as they drive through the ghetto; the poor feel guilty because they condemn themselves as failures. The sad and the sick feel guilty because they suspect that they are a burden on someone; the active and successful also feel guilty because they should be giving time to their families. Divorced people have a whole set of guilt feelings.

A guilty person won't trust others because he doesn't feel trustworthy himself. Very often guilt masquerades as loneliness. There's a difference between loneliness and solitude. A guilty person does not love himself and so he cannot stand solitude. The love-starved are very often carrying a load of guilt because guilty people do not love. The best self is always passing judgment on the worst self. A guilty person dares not love because to love is to reveal the soul and he doesn't dare take that risk. A guilty person cannot really love because the heart of love is trust, and a guilty person doesn't even fully and thoroughly trust himself. Guilt will keep you from having the full and beautiful healings of body and mind and affairs that are available to you. What do you do? You must learn to forgive yourself.

I think another devil that we create is the devil of pessimism. This devil creates its own hell in which we'll suffer forever until we get over it — a hell of fear, anxiety, tension and depression. It arises from giving power to negative possibilities. We look out there and feel like nothing good is going to happen; that we could work hard and rise all the way up to mediocre. The devil of pessimism keeps many of us from being the kind of person we're intended to be.

There's a devil called greed. You see some people driven by greed. Oddly enough, its hell is poverty, lack and limitation. It happens whenever we declare to ourselves, "There's not enough to go around" or "I've got to get mine." And the emphasis is on getting and holding. That shuts off the flow.

Another devil is jealousy. "Why did he get that promotion?" "Why did she get that fur coat and not me?"

There's a devil of procrastination. First, it turns our heads over our shoulders to look back and produces guilt for jobs undone and opportunities not taken. Naturally, that creates a certain feeling of limitation today. Then it turns us to look ahead and burdens us down with a workload that seems to stretch out endlessly. Why? Because we haven't taken care of today.

There are more people who would rather have sympathy than to be a winner — because they feel they can't be a winner. The next best thing is to have sympathy. It's just wonderful to have someone say, "Ah, you poor dear." We just wallow in that stuff, you know. We put a pained expression on our faces, smile weakly but bravely, put up a brave front in spite of it all and let others sympathize with us. Of course, it doesn't change a thing. But it gives us an excuse for failure and mediocrity, whether it's in our work, home, raising our children, social life or whatever. We have a dandy built-in excuse for not succeeding in any of these areas. We lay the blame somewhere else so that we can go scot-free.

If your experience has been unhappy, unrewarding and unfulfilling, what excuse have you been making? Who have you blamed it on? Where have you put the responsibility?

If you don't like your life or some aspect of it, change it! Don't sit around and brood; don't talk a good game and do nothing about it. Change it by changing your thoughts about yourself, about God, about the Devil, about the world and your place in it. We need to cast the devils out. When the devils are gone, we can refill our minds and transform our beliefs with an awareness of the greater possibility that lies asleep in most of us — waiting to be aroused and put to work.

10
DON'T DRAG
ALONG YOUR PAST

What are you going to let hang over in your life from the past? This next year is going to be almost identical to your past one unless you do something about it. There are probably some good things that have happened to you. Let some of that flavor hang over into today. The point is, how many of us are going to carry over some of the things that are not so pleasant and not so good?

How many of us remember how we got our feelings hurt? How many remember criticisms that we've given or received, animosities, angers, a get-even spirit, misunderstandings, resentments or fears? How many of those things are going to color and flavor our lives now?

You see, our todays are made up of a thousand yesterdays strung on the beads of memory, and they will be repeated if we carry them along. They will repeat with monotonous regularity unless we decide that it really is time to change. We have only right *now* — we know that, yet we don't always live like it. There's no way we can live one second of yesterday or one second of tomorrow — only this second right now.

Bring this sharply into focus: you cannot get nor give, you cannot love nor hate, you cannot enjoy nor fight, you cannot be happy nor change your ways tomorrow — only *now*. Whatever you plan to be or do or have, it obviously has to be in the *now*. Your creative mind can create only in the *now*, create only what you give it *now* to do. So we can only accept and believe so that we might begin to change our future *now*.

We have a tendency to inject time lapse or time lag into our thoughts and even into our prayers. We say, "I affirm that everything is going to be all right." Now, the very fact that you said "going to be" is exactly what the creativity of mind picks up, and it reproduces for you "going to be." So you're always chasing that will-o'-the-wisp that you never can catch up to. You have to affirm that "now things are all right" or "they are now becoming."

I'm not saying that it isn't important to plan for tomorrow — it is. But you have to do it now, and it has to be with an idea that you're doing it now. Yesterday's woes have some importance because they are involved in what we are today — if we don't let those yesterdays mold our consciousness and our thought into a pattern of bad yesterdays and then allow those yesterdays to limit us as to what we are implanting in the fertile fields of our mind now.

There isn't any magic or any luck that can change anything overnight or even over a period of time. It's going to happen when you and I do something positive and direct about whatever we want to change. We live life something like a brick mason lives it. We build this morning on what was left over last night. We begin exactly there, you see, unless we do something special about it. We build into the structure of our life exactly what we're thinking in this moment. Tomorrow, it will be there for everyone to see.

You can pretend to be a neat, spiritually minded, fantastic guy, but the trouble is that everyone can look at your life and see whether you are or are not and whether you're really doing the things you talk about. There's no way you can be a hypocrite.

We seem to take one of two approaches to life. One approach is that we are victims of our birth and victims of opportunity. . . or the lack of it. We feel that there is some outside reason why opportunity never quite came to us. We're victims of our location or of our education. What do we do? Very often, we just resignedly make the best of it. The best seems to be no more than to be moderately successful, happy and healthy. Now if that's all we want, that's fine, but that's the best that can happen to us if we feel that life is in control of us. We rebel occasionally when we feel like that, but it's a rather hopeless rebellion.

The other approach is to fight it. That's rather admirable in a way if perhaps a couple of ingredients were added — for instance, when and what to fight. Too often, while we're fighting life, we have a deep feeling that life is an enemy and we have to fight it in order to survive. We tilt at windmills and we fight men of straw that we have created ourselves.

I am sure that if you and I were really positive that there is a better way and we could win in this game of life, we'd try it.

First of all, we have to define what life is. We don't understand how a chick can grow inside an egg and peck its way out. We can watch the process, but we have no idea why it happens. We don't know why a seed can fall into the ground, germinate and become a flower.

It is obvious that there is life and that life is intelligent. We say that there is an Infinite Presence that has consciousness, intelligence and volition. There are evidences of it everywhere. Out of endless possibilities, this intelligence delivers to each of us as much of itself as we are able to accept. Then you begin to understand that life can be much broader and bigger than perhaps you have ever imagined.

You live your life; nobody can live any portion of that life for you. In fact, we really wouldn't want anyone to. We want to make our own mistakes and we want to have our own successes. We must learn to be free and happy in our own minds, and to the degree that we're able to do this, we shall experience a deepening quality and an expanding quality of life.

You don't have to wait to be happy. You don't have to wait until you get out of the house and away from your parents, get through high school or college, get married or have a certain amount of money in the bank. There isn't anything we need to wait for when we understand the basic principle of life: the infinite intelligence and power of this universe is operative in us to the degree that we will accept.

It means that we're going to have to drop the carry-overs that we've had from negative experiences in the past. We need to drop our guilt, our shame and our fears that came out of past experiences. We need to drop negative mental conditioning that we have created and permitted. These things keep us from expressing our perfect life.

I would caution you to quit trying to understand why you did certain things and why negative things happened to you in the past. All you are doing is digging into the garbage of negative things and you'll get it all over you again.

I think we ought to use the past much the same as science uses it. Bring to the present out of the past only that which has some value today.

Start feeling that you are a new person, now. You're not the same person you were back there. Since every cell in your body changes every 11 months, you're not even the same physical person you were 11 months ago. Start knowing and feeling that you are this new person and that those things that happened to the old person don't belong to you because you're *not* the same person. Bang the door on the past, walk away from that door in a new direction and leave all that junk back there where it belongs.

11
YOUR RIGHT TO RICHES

Of all the problems we have, probably the most prevalent one for the greatest number of people is the one of
prosperity, of being successful — a matter of flow of money.
Some of the generally accepted ideas about prosperity are:
money is hard to come by; you have to work your you-
know-what off to get money; money is wrong and it's wrong to
want to be wealthy.

The church has told us "poverty equals piety" until we
have come to believe it. We feel selfish and greedy if we find
ourselves desiring material things in this world and we feel
we're not spiritual if we want money. Actually, the man who
doesn't have much is probably far more materialistically
minded than the man who has plenty. As Ernest Holmes
said, "If you insist that poverty and goodness come in the
same capsule, I'd like to have you explain to me why a hungry
man is more saintly than a well-fed man." If a little money is
all right, why isn't more money all right? Where is the
dividing line? Where on the scale do you arrive at the point
when suddenly the money you need turns into something
bad? It's like saying a little happiness is good, but too much is
terrible.

We discredit both God and ourselves by poverty, lack
and limitation. I am convinced that poverty is a sin. It creates
a form of hell because it blinds man to God's unlimited
supply for him. We are here to express that life, and you
cannot tell me that lack, limitation and poverty help us to
express that life more beautifully. It just doesn't work that

way. Poverty is dirty and poverty is degrading. It fills our prisons; it makes thieves and murderers out of people. It drives people to drink, dope, suicide, delinquency and crime. It's all so unnecessary.

We need to rid ourselves forever of a sneaky feeling that God withholds and that He's pleased with us when we don't have much. The Bible does not recommend poverty. There is no God who is testing us to see how much we can take. God is not limiting us. Nothing witholds our good from us but our own ignorance. We are doing the withholding. Everything for our good has already been provided.

There is plenty of evidence that at the minimum man can have enough money and wherewithal to be able to do what he wants to do when he wants to do it. That's my definition of prosperity. You know $400 skillion in the bank is not going to make me any happier than enough to do what I want to do when I want to do it.

Man has a right to be rich — a divine right to be rich. We are not put here to have a little bit of all the good stuff in this world. There is a lot of prosperity. There are a lot of good things in this world. Who do you think it's for? Do you think it's for a few lucky ones, a few smart ones, a few that trample on other's heads or pull crooked deals? Why do you think all of the abundance of God is in this world? Man has a divine right to be rich. He can have more than just a little taste here and there of the good of this universe.

Not only does man have a right to be rich, he has a responsibility to be rich, to have abundance flowing in his life — this is life expressing itself.

There are two basic principles of true prosperity. The first is that we've got to know better than we've ever known before that life is for us, and it is for us unconditionally. You

don't have to meet certain kinds of conditions before life will
be for you. Life is already for you. God is already for you.
Truth is already for you. God has already provided; it has
been freely given and it is available unto you right now, this
moment and every moment. All of that good that has been
provided is awaiting your recognition, your acceptance and
your use.

Your wealth and your prosperity do not depend on
anything outside of you. You don't have to wait for old Aunt
Martha to die and leave you a bundle. It does not depend on
any person, any place, any thing, any circumstance or any
condition. Appearances have nothing to do with this flow of
good in your life.

We go up and down with the stock market and the
times, in our consciousness. I would point out to you that
many have made fortunes right in the midst of the kinds of
things we often let color our consciousness with limitation
thus keeping us from experiencing our good. I'm pointing
out to you that this good, this flow of good is as available to
you as it is to anyone in this universe if you will learn to have a
wealth consciousness instead of a consciousness of need or
lack. There are no favorites, you see.

The second point is that our limitations in this area are
self-imposed. There is a story about the man who was stand-
ing along the river watching another guy catch quite a
number of fish. The guy threw back all the good-sized fish.
When he would catch a fingerling, he'd keep it. Finally the
man went over and said, "You know it's none of my business,
but I'm curious as to why you throw all those good fish back
and keep these fingerlings."

And the guy replied, "Because I have a small frying
pan."

We accept a little bit because we have a small consciousness. Somehow we feel that we shouldn't have much and we're not worthy, and we are continually selling ourselves short. We have developed a subconscious assumption of limitation and that we have to live with it.

Let's do a little experiment. Imagine that you have before you a sheet of typing paper. On that paper I want you mentally to draw a circle. Now, let me ask you, how big is that circle? Did you go as wide as the paper would allow or maybe even outside of it? Or is the circle about a medium-sized circle or even a small one? That is a pretty solid indication of your own consciousness, of what you think about yourself and your life — whether your consciousness is expansive or whether it's limited.

Now make a dot mentally in the middle of that circle that you drew. That dot in the middle represents you. Now, mentally take an eraser and erase the circle so you have only the dot left. Now, we're getting a picture of what you really are. Life is that big to you.

Now look at the faint outline of that circle that you have erased — you can still see it there. What are the limitations that you've been placing on yourself that caused you to draw a circle that size? Do you have in your consciousness things like: It can't be done, I'll never have enough money, my job is my security and it just doesn't pay that much, I'm too young or too old, I need more education? Do you feel your present circumstances are such that there's no way you could have wealth, or you'd like to have more of the abundant things of this world but you don't know how to get them? Are those the kinds of things that have been in your mind? Honestly ask yourself and look at yourself — what has kept you from demonstrating more abundance in life? These limitations in and of themselves have no validity in your life except as you think them and give them validity. You *can* erase that circle that you have created around yourself.

As you contemplate that dot, recognize that you are an individualized center of life in a limitless universe. Nothing is withheld from you. The circle that you drew was your circle. You drew your own limitations, but you also can erase them. It doesn't do any good to mentally erase that circle on the paper if you don't also mentally erase those limitations that caused the circle in the first place.

How do you erase these psychological barriers and become more expansive? There are a lot of things you can do and some of them may sound simple to you, but you can use anything that will help you get rolling in the direction of a higher, greater, wealth-minded consciousness. Of course, first and most important is the fact that you have to know better than you've ever known before that you are part of God. You are part of infinite wealth. When you know that, you cannot be part of poverty, limitation and need because God is wealth. You need to ask yourself from that standpoint: how much am I worth? Your answer to that is what life will give you.

There is a law in this universe that says, "That which you can conceive of, believe in and confidentially expect must necessarily become part of your experience." The people who have more than you have, have learned consciously or unconsciously to use that law to a greater degree. Learn, then, to get a wealth consciousness going for you.

Another thing to do is to get used to the feel of money. Many people unconsciously are afraid of money. If someone walked up to you and tried to hand you a $100 bill, you would probably back off. We need to see money for what it is. It's friendly, great, creates all kinds of good in this world and is a flowing thing in your life. Open up the gates and let it flow.

Start to think in larger terms. I know a man who is now a millionaire. I asked him how he got that way and he said, "I used to think in hundreds. Then as the hundreds began to pile in, I began to add a zero or two and I began to think in thousands. Now, I think in millions and it's exactly the same thing. I can't tell the difference. I just think in bigger numbers, that's all." Numbers are merely a convenience, you know, but we let them become a limitation to us. If you have a few dollar bills in your billfold, look at them and imagine several more zeros behind them. Some people recommend carrying around a $100 bill — you don't spend it, you just have it and you look at it and feel wealthy.

Make a notebook and put pictures on each page for as many things as you want. Describe it in writing, since looking at it and reading about it involves more of your senses. You'll begin to accept this thing as belonging to you.

Mingle with success. Mingle as much as you can with people who are already successful — just to get the feeling. Go into neighborhoods where the best homes are and feel comfortable. I remember when I was having such a struggle, I used to drive through Beverly Hills. I would not let it make me feel little; I would feel that this is where I belong. I never did a specific treatment about that but I did end up living in Beverly Hills through a strange set of circumstances.

The people who are as poor as you, or poorer, haven't anything to contribute to your consciousness. As much as you can, mingle with the people who are successful and who have money — let the feeling rub off on you. Feel that you belong with them. Go to the best stores, touch the merchandise and feel that this is the kind of place where you buy your things.

When you go to sleep at night, say to yourself, "I am wealth and because I am wealth, I am wealthy." See if your consciousness doesn't start to change.

Bless what you have. I don't care how little it is, bless it. If you keep feeling that it's not enough and you're critical of the fact that you don't have enough, it'll shrivel on you. Bless what you have, even if it doesn't seem like enough, and watch it grow. That which you bless will bless you back.

Every day find a quiet place where you can relax and shut out the problems of your day and your life. See and feel yourself with all that it takes to make life rich and worthwhile. Visualize yourself in the midst of that, doing what you like to do and doing it successfully, happily and prosperously. Visualize yourself with all of your debts paid and with enough money left over for all your needs and the extras you would enjoy. Gain a sense of God pouring through you as ideas, opportunities and unexpected good that you hadn't even thought about. Do this until you begin to believe it. Write an affirmation of abundance and read it during the day. Read it especially in the morning to set your tone for the day. Read it at night near the time you go to sleep so that it's fresh on your mind and can soak in all night. Eliminate the pollution that's been accumulating from all those ridiculous ideas you've been told. Eliminate that pollution and recycle your thought into something more nearly the truth about you.

You might affirm something like this: I am relaxed, I am open and receptive to my prosperity. I know it is right for me, so I no longer feel guilty about my search for successful living. Every day I am healthier, happier, more prosperous and more successful. Propserity comes to me now and remains with me always.

Once you begin to believe this affirmation, the creative medium at the subconscious level will take that and begin to reproduce it for you just as easily as it has produced lack, need and limitation in your life.

One more thing: be a giver. You cannot lose by giving. My dad used to say, "You can't outgive God." Give freely; don't give because you feel you have to or you won't get anything back. Give because you know there is a flow of life and if you let it out at one end, it'll come in the other. Life will replace with increase whatever you give. Give freely to any worthwhile project; you cannot lose. All of us want to get. Oh, we love to get! But we're afraid to give because we're afraid there won't be any more. There really is no prosperity in that kind of consciousness, none at all.

You have a divine right to riches because of who you are — a child of the King. You're a part of God. Develop your own consciousness. You can't make it happen, but you can make your mind behave. You can let wealth flow through your life.

12
TO YOUR GOOD HEALTH

We seek health. It starts with a deep conviction that it's normal to be healthy. The proper kind of thought, thinking the right kinds of things, stirring up the right kinds of responses and emotions can release and let that built-in physician take over and let normalcy become our way of life. Nothing hinders us but our lack of acceptance.

We ought to become aware of the things that we do to ourselves that deprive us of our health. Our thoughts and our emotions affect the heart, disgestive system, the working of the glands and all the various things that go on in our bodies. It has been proved that not only functional disorders are caused by thoughts and emotions, but even organic and structural difficulties are created by ourselves.

If thought can inhibit the activity of the body and cause us to be ill, thought turned around can let this body be healthy and well. No miracles have to take place, the miracle is already here. All we have to do is get out of the way and let it do its thing.

We do this with prayer, spiritual mind treatment, and that is not for the purpose of getting God to do some fantastic miracle but to change something in the way we've been thinking — to effect a change in our thought so that we can let the normal perfection take place.

We don't consciously create disease, but we condition our body by our thoughts so that it becomes host to bugs and germs. We have all kinds of germs and microbes in our bodies all the time. Something triggers their activity and suddenly they take over and create an illness. What triggers that? Our own consciousness has inhibited the flow of perfection of life.

You and I may well ask ourselves, "What is my verdict about me? Have I decided to be sick or to be well, or a little of each?" Every organ and every function of your body is directly related to the brain through the two nervous systems — the central and the autonomic. Messages from this brain are sent to every part, to every organ, to every function of the body. What we're thinking is important because the body is going to respond one way or the other to these signals that are sent from the brain. Our patterns of thought so condition our bodies as to either welcome or reject such things as infectious disease.

I listened to a tape by Dr. Simonton, an M.D. who has become somewhat of an expert in the field of cancer. Along with radiation and other things that medical doctors do, he is using meditation and having a fantastic cure rate. He says that every one of us has had cancer probably a thousand times or more in our lives. But the immune mechanism in the body recognized it, ran out there and killed it off. Apparently our patterns of thinking were such that it could not take hold.

Health appears to rest on three things: (1) Common sense care of the body — proper foods, proper amount of rest and those kinds of things. (2) The verdict that you have reached mentally as to what the state of your health shall be. (3) The ability to realize that in spite of whatever evidence, whatever other verdicts have been made about your condition, you may render a new verdict anytime you decide to do so.

You may render the kind of verdict you want and when you do this, your body will respond. That healing presence, the power and presence of God within you, immediately will accept your new verdict and begin to work on that to bring your body, your mind, your emotions and your affairs into proper perspective and into perfect health. You are one with God, and God is not sick. If the real of you is God, and God is not sick, then the real of you cannot be sick.

What impairs your health? The basic cause has to be destructive patterns of thought. It isn't just thinking of disease that causes disease. Thought patterns that include fear, anxiety, tension, worry, anger, frustration have a deleterious effect upon the body, and the body responds to that.

There are some of us who are slowly committing suicide by the destructive, constricting patterns of thought that we carry from day to day. We must stop beating ourselves up physically by our damaging thoughts and unwise physical activities.

But no condition can be healed if it is caused by something that the individual will not give up. If you put your hand on a hot stove, the first thing you need to do is to remove your hand from the stove. Now, you can pray until you turn blue, you can give all kinds of excuses, but nothing will help until you give up putting your hand on the stove.

If tension and stress and those other things are taking their toll in your body by creating physical ailments, no outer cure can work until whatever caused it is removed, given up and taken away. Don't expect a healing of your body if you're not willing to do your part.

We know that there is a guiding intelligence within us, and it can tell us what to do and how to do it if we'll listen. Sometimes I think we almost deliberately and stubbornly hang on to some negative pattern of thought and suffer the consequences anyway, feeling that perhaps we can get away with it, which obviously we cannot. So, on this basis, I would ask you, "Are you blocking your own health and your own healing?" Nothing else and no one else can block that for you.

Search your own heart and mind about this. There may be habits you will have to break. There may be habits you will have to form. But there's an intelligence that will help you know and pinpoint these things. There may be people whom you will have to forgive and release, because that probably is one of the greatest single causes of problems in our lives. If you will earnestly and sincerely search your own mind until you discover those things that need to be changed in your own consciousness, then the healing presence will begin to release healing power throughout your body.

We expect to be sick. We get up in the morning and say (we belong to the "Symptom-a-Day Club"), "Where am I sick today?" If there isn't anything the matter, we'll by-george fix up something pretty quick. I might ask you this: Do you want to be healed or do you just want to quit hurting? There's quite a difference, you know.

You can establish a health pattern within you instead of an illness pattern of thinking. That is totally and completely up to you. Take your mind off the things that have created problems within you. Put your mind on the kinds of things that will create a pure and healing consciousness within you that will result in a pure and healing activity within your body, mind and affairs.

In my own ministry, I have seen healings of all sorts: relationships, affairs and everything else. I have seen such so-called minor things as the instant healings of colds, flu and headaches. But I have also seen healings of major illnesses. A lady, about 30 years old, whose fingers were all gnarled with arthritis, came to me. She used two crutches, her feet were turned in, and she walked on her ankles. I watched as those fingers and ankles straightened out; I could hear it happening. She walked out of my office without those crutches 10 years ago and she is without them today.

I saw a man who had a severe heart attack and had been released from his government job. We had a spiritual mind treatment for his healing. He didn't know he was healed until about two weeks later when he found himself running up and down the basement stairs. He said to himself, "My God! I'm not supposed to do that." Then with his next breath, "I'm well!" He went to his doctor, had an examination and was told that they found nothing wrong with him. He was reinstated on his job which he held until he retired recently.

How does all of this happen? It happens through prayer, spiritual mind treatment. We turn mentally from the problem. Our big problem in prayer for healing is that we have said, "Oh God, cure this dear lady of this horrible cancer that's eating up her vitals." Now, where is our attention, our faith, our focus? On the cancer, right? As long as we do this, we're giving attention to something we say doesn't belong. So, we turn mentally away from the illness. We do not say the illness does not exist. We don't say that it's a figment of the imagination. We're aware that there is something to be healed or we wouldn't need a healing. But then, once aware of the problem, we give it no place in our consciousness.

We affirm, believe and visualize the truth. The truth is perfection, God's perfection, moving in the body. This is the power that heals and it's in the cells of your body and mind, right now, waiting to do its thing when we stop inhibiting it.

A spiritual mind treatment begins and ends in the mind. If you heal the body but don't heal the mind, then the mind's going to make it sick again. We don't have to create health, you see. We have to get rid of the stuff that stops that perfection from acting, from taking place. Healing can take place in you right now, today, this very moment. You can do it now; you can let it happen.

13
THE MAGIC POWER OF LOVE

It's a paradox of our times: there is so much talk about love and so much confusion about the meaning of it. The very word itself has an overused feeling and has lost its meaning. We tend to back off from "love" and say, "I don't want to get involved" or "I need to keep my feet on the ground and not let my emotions run away with me." But holding back love does not fulfill our needs. We lack what would make us whole and we instinctively know this. The so-called "common man" has within him a great storehouse of tenderness that he is afraid to turn loose.

If we would probe deeply enough, we would find that real love, the giving and the receiving of real unadulterated love, is the dream of every man and every woman. See how hard we try to reach others, to awaken an understanding and to get a response because no one of us is complete all by himself. It is a poor, forlorn human being who does not and has not at least experienced a moment of an all-consuming love.

Pulpits and editorials are saying we should love one another, but how can we do that when almost everyone is a competitor in one way or another? We are told not to mix business with pleasure, friendship, family and love, but they get mixed in spite of the directive. If these kinds of things dilute business a little, business manages to dilute pleasure, friendship, family and love a lot. Making a living seems to be the most important thing today and tends to exclude a pure, flowing, completely giving love.

We've made the mistake of thinking of love as a weak thing — a little emotion, an effeminate little frill to life — and that tenderness, gentleness, thoughtfulness and unselfishness equate themselves with weakness. But that's not so. It takes a strong person to be gentle.

We seem to have fallen on a cold, hard cynical age. We're afraid to express our true feelings and our true emotions. A man said to me, "Well, she should know I love her without my having to say so. Don't I go out and work to bring home the money?" But you know he'd do the same thing if he hired a housekeeper. Love is more than just earning a living or cleaning the house and washing dirty socks. Yes, those are things that are sometimes done out of love but they do not constitute the feeling and power of love, nor are they a substitute for love.

In our scientific age, it's difficult to love because it isn't something you can learn out of a textbook or through watching television. You can't do it electronically or through a computer. Love is not goodwill, tolerance or a rational belief. Sometimes it actually defies all rhyme and reason. Love is an essence, a fabric woven into the universe. Because it's a part of us, it's demanding. Love is not always comfortable, and it's not meant to be. It demands a giving of the self. Sometimes our self-image is so low that unconsciously we don't feel that we have that much to give, so we settle for something less.

Love makes us very vulnerable. We don't want to be ignored, ridiculed or rejected. If we really love, we run the risk of that, so we don't allow ourselves the vulnerability of love. We would rather feel safe than know the precarious wonders of real, honest, beautiful, giving love.

We throw up the barrier of bargaining. We love those

who can do something for us. Do you know that there are people who are so hungry for love that even counterfeit love can persuade them? It's the tool of some con men, because we are hungry to give and receive love. There's scarcely one of us who has not used love as a bargaining agent, as a weapon, with our children or our spouse. We give and withhold in order to get what we want. We expect to be loved because we have done something. Our children should love us because we have sacrificed in order to raise them.

Now it's possible, I know, to win love under such false pretenses, but it's impossible to hold it. It will not hold steady because other people need love, too. Some people never seem to develop the ability to love and to give, and the whole problem is that they've been too busy trying to get someone to love them. They feel like they have lots of love to give, but they don't give it until they find someone who will give it back.

We often fail to give love for three reasons: (1) We're afraid of rejection, (2) we have a sneaky feeling that we really don't have any love to give and (3) we're selfish — we want to receive and we will not give until we are receiving. This failure springs from a sense of separateness and isolation. The oneness with God and the universe is not recognized.

We are told that God is love, not God has love or is loving. Thus, at the very center of your being where God is, is love. Not that you *have* love, but that you *are* love. That love within each one of us cries out for expression. Why does it do that? We have this desperate need to love and to be loved because we all are parts of God and those parts are crying out in longing to be one again.

Man has found all kinds of ways to separate himself from others, life and God. Too many of us are love-blocked. The channels of our hearts and minds are clogged and dammed up through our own selfishness. Too often when we reach out to touch someone, we do it only to receive and not to give, to know that they are physically there. If we would truly touch, we must also truly touch with our minds, hopes, dreams, desires and our givingness. If we could let ourselves go in that touch, we would discover that we not only have touched someone else, but we have touched God. Something new would begin to happen because something deeper would take place in us.

The one who lets love and compassion flow through him, unimpeded, will be showered with love and compassion in return. It may not be from that particular individual, but from somewhere, because what you give, you will receive.

Another thing we do is to pick and choose who it is we're going to love and who our love is going to go out to. Obviously this picking and choosing has cut us off from some beautiful experiences we might otherwise have had. We must come to that point where we love simply because we can't help but love. We must relate in love and trust and forgiveness, no matter who it is. Every person is God expressing himself in some unique way. That's true of every person no matter how shabby that appearance might be from the human standpoint. Whether or not another person is aware of who and what he is, we must reflect that awareness of God in our respect, our trust and our love for them.

Too often we are not aware of God in others; love is only a surface emotion between two people. Rather than reaching into the all-consuming love stored within another human being, we look at only surface traits: good looks, nice clothes, winning personality and popularity. This is especially true when two people "fall in love." But surface love will not survive in a marriage. When the glamor wears off and faults are discovered, they find that there was no deep love involved. They find that marriage is not a 50/50 proposition. It turns out to be a 100/100 proposition. Each spouse must give deeply of his love if he wishes to have that love returned. Each one can't go only half-way. What would happen if each person only went 48% of the way — what's going to fill that other 4%? If each one can give everything he has to his spouse, then he doesn't have to worry about what he is going to get in return.

Each person has faults, including you. Have you ever tried to see the good in your spouse? Quit looking at the faults and talking about them. If you would quit talking about the faults and start talking and thinking about the good qualities, you might discover you have invented for yourself a pretty good mate and a happy fulfilling marriage. Find the good and love that. There is a genuine, beautiful experience of love that, rightly understood, will heal, bless and change your marriage.

Let's look at the components that make up love, as Paul pointed them up in I Corinthians 13 whether it is love of your spouse, children, neighbors, family or the strangers that you come in contact with.

The first component is patience. Love obviously knows that there is no power as great and so it can afford to wait. If you're impatient, it means that you're not fully expressing love.

Along that same line, love is not easily provoked. We have a tendency to look at bad temper as a kind of harmless weakness, but it is far removed from true love. We have no right to weigh one another's sins; we have no right to look at and criticize people's motives. We also cannot be touchy and overly sensitive, because that rises out of an ego that has not grown up yet. Over-sensitivity is caused by too much interest in the self.

The second component of love is kindness. Jesus spent a lot of time just being kind. He didn't look for any return; he just was interested in making people happy. How do you do when it comes to kindness? Why aren't we more kind? What are we afraid of? It pays back so abundantly and it costs so very little. How long has it been since you were just plain kind? How kind are you to the waitress in the restaurant? How kind are you to the clerk in the store? How kind are you to the people who can be of no service to you whatever?

The third component is givingness. Givingness goes out and gives and returns again without any hope of return. I remember one time my daughter unexpectedly gave me a big kiss. You know what I said? I said, "What was that for?" She answered, "Because I love you."

Envy arises from a feeling of competition, that someone has something you want or is going to get something you want. But givingness as a part of love is generous and it rejoices in all good for everyone. How well do you do when someone achieves what you want to achieve? How honestly and generously do you give of your love and appreciation and rejoice with all good no matter who has it?

Point four: humility. This is not the doormat type of thing where you let everyone wipe their feet on you, but this is the kind of thing that has a quiet inner strength. Humility in love goes out in strength and gives because it can't help it. We say, "Oh, I'll never do something for him again. I did all that and he never even said 'thank you'." We like to be thanked, but that's a small way to look at it. Do you give in order to get some kind of return or do you give with humility because that's your nature?

The fifth component is courtesy. Love cannot bring hurt to someone else merely for some kind of self-gratification. A loving person, a truly loving person, is accepted anywhere. Why is it that we are more courteous to everyone else than we are to the people we say we love the most?

Component number six: unselfishness. Why do you love? Do you have to have a reason? Do you have to have a return? Or do you love simply because that's what you are, and your love has to flow like the sun has to shine? Why do you love your husband? Because he goes to work and brings home money so you have a roof over your head? Why do you love your wife? Because she washes and cooks and sews (and maybe also goes to work and brings home the money to buy the groceries)? Can you love the unlovable? There isn't any particular virtue in loving the lovable — anyone can do that. Make a project this week of loving someone who's not lovable, as far as you're concerned. Every day bless him and send your sincere and honest love to him.

Number seven: sincerity. Did you ever notice that the people who influence you the most are those who believe in you? They're not suspicious of your motives. Do we have to look for some kind of motive? You know the joke about the husband who brings home the flowers and the wife immediately think he's been up to something. If you're suspicious of people and watching out so you can't get taken, you will get taken.

How many of these components are you falling short on? It's not easy to do anything about our inhibitions and our prides that we have built up within ourselves over the years.

We sometimes forget that love is more what we are than what we do. If we can drop our pride and fear, we will come to know that truly the greatest power in this world is love. It can transform the least of us into the greatest. I wonder how many of us have really known the absolute joy of totally giving ourselves away in an all-consuming love that holds nothing back.

14
PRACTICE IMMORTALITY

There are times when people ask me, "Do you really believe in immortality? If so, do you believe that all people are immortal?" I think that immortality has been proved in a number ways. To me, there is no question about this. I believe that we're all destined to live forever. If one person is immortal, then obviously all people are immortal because we're all out of the same cloth. The life we are now experiencing is the life of God in us, and that life is eternal. We're not just a little isolated hunk of driftwood on the sea of life. We are an integral part, we are made out of God-stuff, out of the life of this universe. That's why we're eternal.

There are some psychically oriented people who claim to have observed the separation of the spirit from the body. I don't know whether they did or not; I've never seen it. More common are the people who have communicated with those whom we say have departed. I was impressed when Bishop Pike, the Episcopalian Bishop, communicated with his son who had departed this experience. There used to be so many things I wouldn't believe; there was a day when if I couldn't touch it, taste it, feel it, see it or smell it, I didn't believe it. Life has proved to me that almost everything that I doubted has turned out to be true.

For quite a few years in another church, I spent the bulk of my time getting people ready to die. Isn't that dandy? Getting people ready to die! In fact, I would quote John Wesley in stentorian tones, "Watch our people die," or say, "Our people die well." The people who are always getting ready to die never really live. Those people who are doing the living, never really die; they merely shift the scene.

Death can be viewed from either side. It's like the sailing ship with all its beautiful sails. It pulls out from the shore, and the people say, "There she goes." They watch it until it's just a speck on the horizon and then it's gone. But over on the other shore, people see that little speck. It grows and comes closer. The people say, "There she comes."

We're human. This thing that we call death happens to our friends and our loved ones, and there's an empty spot in our hearts and our lives. We miss them, we miss their physical presence. When we begin to understand immortality and the ongoingness of life, we will see that death is but a gateway to a larger life.

Is death really an enemy? Actually, it's our feelings about death that happen to be the real enemy. These feelings must be destroyed before we can live fully. The church has fostered many of the superstitious, strange things that we have believed about death.

Death comes only to the body. Death cannot touch you. Nothing can happen to life, and you are life. So, nothing can happen to you. You will always go on being who you are right now, whether you're in this body of flesh or out of it — endlessly unfolding, endlessly expanding into greater and greater experiences of life.

Jesus said that flesh and blood can't enter the Kingdom. I know I'm more than a physical body — I'm made up of the spirit, the soul and the mind. These three can enter the Kingdom of Heaven; they do not die.

Practice — think of yourself as an eternal being, ever-growing, expanding, unfolding, whether in this experience or the next.

15
YOUR QUEST FOR HAPPINESS

Everyone of us desires to be healthy, wealthy and happy, don't we? There is no reason on God's green earth that we should not be healthy, wealthy and happy. We search for happiness, and in this quest, too often we wrongly identify happiness and what brings it. We seek frantically and it's almost laughable — if it weren't so serious — to see some of the frantic things we do trying to find happiness for ourselves. We all experience it in varying degrees.

Often, we seek it in material things, but we find that — in and of themselves, of course — the material things of life do not necessarily bring happiness. I know a man whom I think is eminently successful in just about every way you could imagine that a man could be successful. He said to me one day, "People think I'm great."

I said, "You are great."

He replied, "Then if I'm so great, why am I not happy?"

We usually equate happiness with something we don't have — something exciting, new and different that would just flood us with happiness, such as a new love, a new spouse, a new job, a new location. Too often we put our emphasis on the new, but when the newness wears off, it did not bring happiness permanently. That woman, whom we just had to have for a wife because she was so exciting, gorgeous and wonderful, turns out looking pretty raunchy in the morning. That man, who was the knight in shining armor, understanding, loving and so well-dressed, turns out to have holes in the seat of his drawers. All of a sudden, the newness wears off. Any new activity, if it is beautiful just for its own sake, becomes purposeless, and it fails in doing what we expected it to do in our own lives.

When we have run the gamut of all these things, we realize that things, in and of themselves, do not bring us permanent happiness. In fact, it does seem evident that happiness is not an end in itself to be sought, but rather that it is a by-product. It seems to boil down to *feeling* happy versus *being* happy. We may have to choose between looking for a good time and living a good life.

We're so constituted that stagnation takes happiness away. It's terrible when your life is at its low point and stagnant, but if you work on yourself, climb to some heights of consciousness and stagnate at that level, it's just as stagnant as it was down below.

Unhappiness can be a habit. We get into an unhappiness rut. I know some people who would miss their unhappiness. You've heard them say, "Things are just going too good — it makes me nervous. I wonder what terrible calamity is going to happen to us?"

I know a man who got worried because he didn't have any worries at the moment. That worried him and made him uncomfortable. How many times have you felt at some very high moment that you have no right to be that happy? There seems to be a perverse streak in us that takes delight in wallowing in the mire of despondency and unhappiness.

If you wonder why your life is not as happy as you'd like it to be, step aside from yourself and listen to the things you and other people talk about. Just listen to it — toil, trouble, headaches, heartaches, disappointments, problems on the job, problems in the home, problems with the children and so on. It's a wonder we're as happy as we are. You'll find that seldom are there real expressions of joy, happiness and enthusiasm for living. In fact, if you go around enthusiastic about living, they'll think you're some kind of a nut.

What is happiness? You can't really describe it any more than you can describe any other emotion. But I know some things that happiness accompanies.

One of them is a faith in life, in a higher power. . . a faith in God. That's even true if a person believes God is "up there," remote and removed. If that man finds a way to make peace in his heart with that God up there, he finds a sense of joy and happiness. When we have faith in God within, there's a strength, comfort and happiness in knowing that you are inseparably a part of God.

Without creating a duality in mind, I formed a company — God and Company. I feel that I have all the power, wisdom, strength and all the good of God available to me in this company. You can form a company too.

Another way that will bring happiness is to like yourself regardless of the stupid, dumb, ridiculous things that you have done in the past. You've got to leave those things behind; they have nothing to do with you today, except for any lessons you may have learned. If you don't like yourself, you're not going to feel worthy of happiness, and it's going to escape you every time.

You do not need to be punished anymore. You may have whipped yourself mentally far too long. There is no earthly reason for suffering, nor is there any power in this universe that is able to make you suffer, but you. There is no power that wants to do that unless you use the power of the universe to do something negative to yourself. When you like yourself, you can be more interested in giving love and happiness than you are in receiving it.

Another thing that brings happiness is dedication to a

purpose. That purpose doesn't have to be earthshaking. You see, accomplishing is more important than accomplishment. In other words, the doing is more important than the having done. So be going somewhere — dedicated to a purpose. That will in turn provide worthwhile activities, mental, physical and emotional. You'll be on the move, and when you're on the move, stagnation cannot settle in. As you move, each day brings its little portion of happinesses. You can let life be a constant challenge to you. There is always more good available to you than you have experienced up to this point. Start every day by knowing that today is a better day than yesterday.

Have a vital, lively interest in everything and everyone. Be curious about life. There are so many great, good, interesting, wonderful things all around us that go by us without our noticing. You grow by participating in life. If you want to be an interesting person, be interested.

One more point — like what you do. If you like what you do, you'll be a happy person. Before you can do greater things, you have to like doing whatever it is you're doing. If you hate it, it's very difficult to move into a better position. It's very difficult to move out of where your consciousness is negative into something that's going to be beautiful and positive, because you're taking your consciousness with you.

Learn the pleasure of doing and giving. Learn to be content. Now, I didn't say satisfied. Contentment and satisfaction are two different things. If I'm satisfied, my wheels are going to slow down. If I'm contented, I have a happy mental attitude even though I don't have all that I desire. I want to grow and become more, but I will carry in the present situation a contented spirit because I know I'm going to go beyond the current circumstances.

Let your talent and your ability come forth. This creative spirit within you wants to do some things through you. It may not seem important to the world, but it will be important to you — you'll find your happiness. Do it well and do it lovingly for the sense of accomplishment.

Take pleasure in the little things. There are so many opportunities for happiness that we go right by because we forget to take pleasure in the little things. Be an appreciater because there's so much to appreciate and your spirit will turn from negativity and darkness to happiness and positivity.

Happiness is a state of mind. We know we can control our state of mind if we want to. Start from a feeling of being happy, now. Feel that it comes up from within you and will automatically grow and expand. You will be surprised how different life looks to you when you're working out of a happy state of mind. It will increase your capacity for more and greater happiness.

Smile. You cannot feel depressed and smile at the same time. Try it. It's a happy attitude and spirit that walks with you. Your life will take on dimensions of beauty, joy, happiness and peace.

16
LIFE . . .
THE GREAT ADVENTURE

We seek that which is exciting. When the actual experience is denied us, we find it secondhand. We read about exciting lives in books or see it in movies and on television. But, did you know that the days of adventure, thrill and excitement are not really over? There are some left for you — the thrill and accomplishment of building a whole new life — exciting, worthwhile and fulfilling in every way.

I can hear you saying, "Yuk, if that's excitement — forget it." But I'm not talking about the life you may have been living — humdrum, boring, a battle, a fight, a treadmill with more failures than successes. I'm talking about the life that lies within the reach of you, right now, with all the thrill, the excitement and the satisfaction of doing something at which you are happy in the doing and successful in the completion.

You see, life is not cut and dried. Life is not preplanned beyond our control. For too long, we have been told, and to a great degree we have accepted, that we have to take whatever life dishes out, as though life were a separate entity doing things to us. We feel we are destined by some capricious fate to live a sort of thwarted, mediocre and humdrum existence with toil, sweat and partial success.

In spite of that, we have a feeling that life can be better than this which we are experiencing. This is the same impulsion that created pioneers of every age. It's the impulsion that caused men to come over to the New World and settle this country. It's the same impulsion used to put men on the moon; to find new things in science or to write great literature.

If you'd like to have some fun, excitement and adventure, you must recognize that life does not pick a few for good fortune and high experience and turn its back on the rest.

Life tends to unfold in the exact pattern of your thought about yourself, life in general, your place in life (in relation to other people), your abilities and your capabilities. There is a divine pattern for man — a fuller and greater expression of that which we are. We are evolving, unfolding beings and there is something better for us to experience.

The whole thing is up to you. You're not stuck in the situation where you are. The pattern can be changed, but only you can change it. The universe is for you, not against you. This is a giving universe. All around you is God's good awaiting your acceptance so that it might move through you. Nothing is holding anything back from you but your own limited, negative thinking.

You supply the raw materials that go into making your own life experiences. You feed it into your computer, and the computer kicks it out as life experience. You can change the material that goes into the computer of creativity any time you so desire.

Now, are you ready to go on an exciting adventure? It'll be your own. Are you ready for something new and different? Then it's time to pack and get started. It's time to stop thinking about it and do it. You can start doing it in your mind right this moment, right where you are. It doesn't have to be some day, tomorrow or in the morning. You start on this adventure the moment you decide you're going to start.

You're going to have to leave some things behind. On

the adventure of life, there are some things you cannot pack with you if life is going to open up and unfold for you. You're going to have to leave behind old ways of thinking and reacting. You're going to have to leave behind some faith in hatred, jealously, guilt, limitation and lack, criticism, cruel fate and helplessness. You're going to have to leave behind your self-pity.

There is some courage required and some risk involved because it's risky to leave old comfy patterns of the years. They have become beloved companions — the self-pity and ideas of helplessness. It's risky to break the mold of our thoughts and reactions.

You will want to live with some greater degree of confidence. Confident living does not mean a way free of challenges and free of apparent resistances to your further growth, but rather a way to meet and to handle these exigencies of life.

You will need to regain your perspective. I think having lost that perspective is one of the major enemies of confident living. Things have an importance and worth to us only as we give it some kind of importance and worth. We have a tendency to look only at the immediate.

You will need to learn to trust God and your fellow man. The idea of separateness has given rise to doubt, fear and a sense of aloneness within us all. You will need to be willing to live by faith.

The average lifespan of man is about half a million hours — 500,000 hours. Could you dare to experiment with just 24 of those? If so, could you dare to expand it to 168 hours — one week — out of half a million? Could you turn yourself over totally into living a faith that can develop into something greater than you are, a faith you can live by?

Fasten your faith and begin to believe in nothing but the good and the beautiful and the true despite what your eyes are seeing.

Cultivate the little happinesses until courage begins to return and hope can reach out its fingers a little farther. Look forward to the next moment, to the next hour, to the promise of a nice lunch or dinner, to a good night's sleep. Sink your roots deep into the present until strength begins to grow to the point where you can then think of tomorrow.

Believe in hope. It has something to offer; it enables you to drain the last drop of joy from whatever time you have. Hope that there is something better for you. Hope until it becomes faith. Even if you only have faith for a little at first, the demonstrations in your life will lead to more faith.

Nothing is withheld. If it's good and makes life more expressive and fulfilling, the universe does not hold anything back. You can change your life.

This message is for the men and women who are not ready to stand still, who refuse to cease to grow, who will not stagnate. You can take advantage of the infinite energy within you and all around you. The unpardonable sin, as far as life goes, would be to stand still, to stagnate, to go nowhere. The infinite energy is your energy. The infinite intelligence is your intelligence. The life principle. To live triumphantly in this present day, in this present world, you have but to supply the direction and walk in harmony with this life force that will not be denied its expression. It wants to express itself through you as you, but until you can supply the direction and walk in harmony with it, it can't do much through you.

Here you are with a mind that is able to work with this fantastic vital force of the universe, with all of the intelligence and all of the energy to do anything. The very fact that we have obstacles is in our favor. If we didn't have obstacles to overcome, we'd probably stagnate. There's something about an obstacle that needs to be overcome and it drives us forward.

It doesn't matter if you're a professional, businessman, industrialist, housewife, clerk, a student or whatever; it doesn't matter whether you have millions at your disposal or whether you have any distinction whatever. The greater your need, the more readily it responds to you. It is willing and ready to help you.

No matter how tremendous your problem may be or how simple, the solution lies within yourself. Good, better, best. Where do you want to be? You always decide. You have always decided consciously or unconsciously. Where do you want your life experience to fall? What you decide and what you permit is the way it's going to be for you.